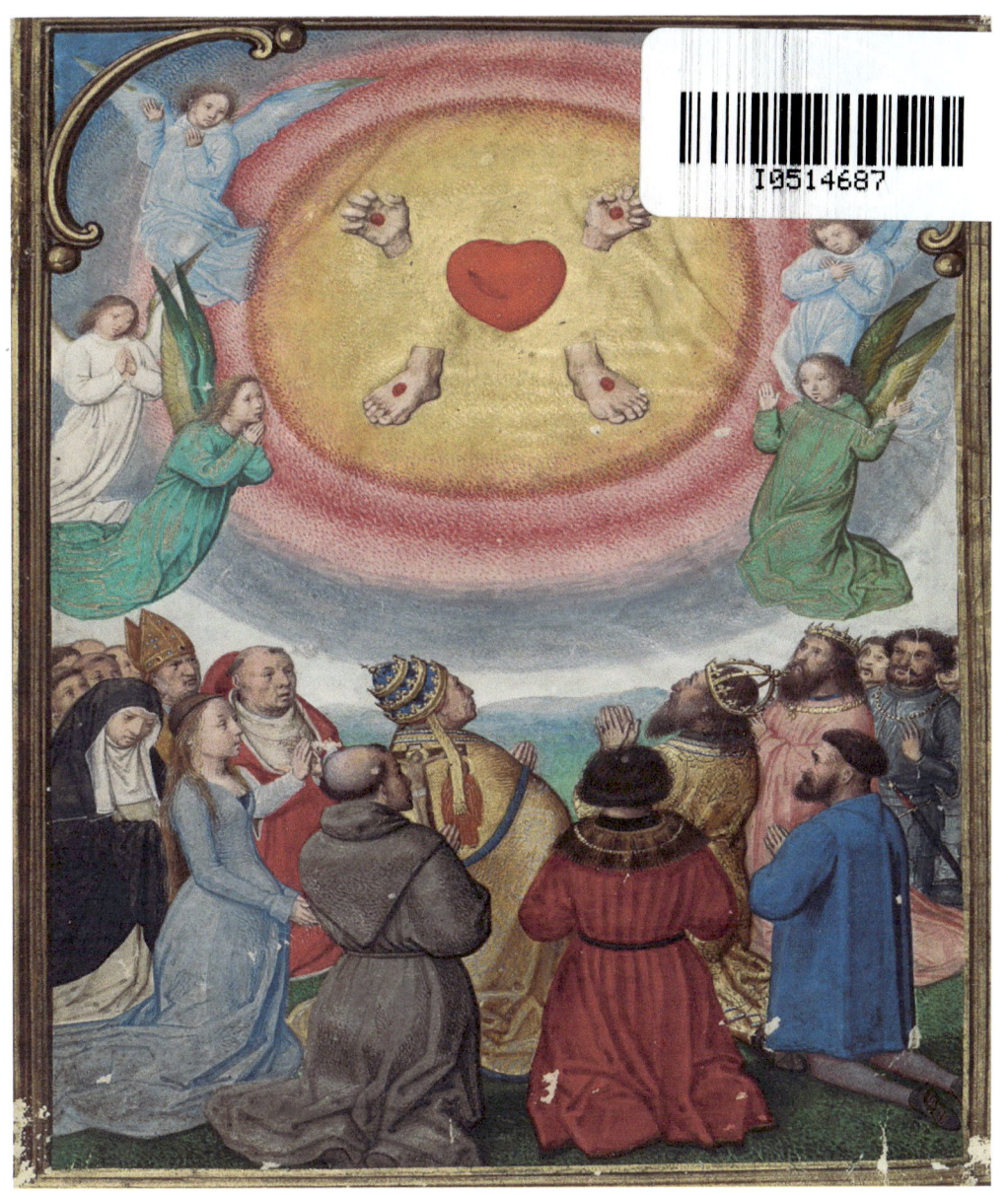

Five Wounds
Photo Chaplet

Cover and interior design copyright © Shalone Cason 2020

Imprimatur: Edmundus Surmont, Vicarius Generalis 1909

Check out our other products and books at casoncatholic.com
And please leave a review on Amazon
God bless +

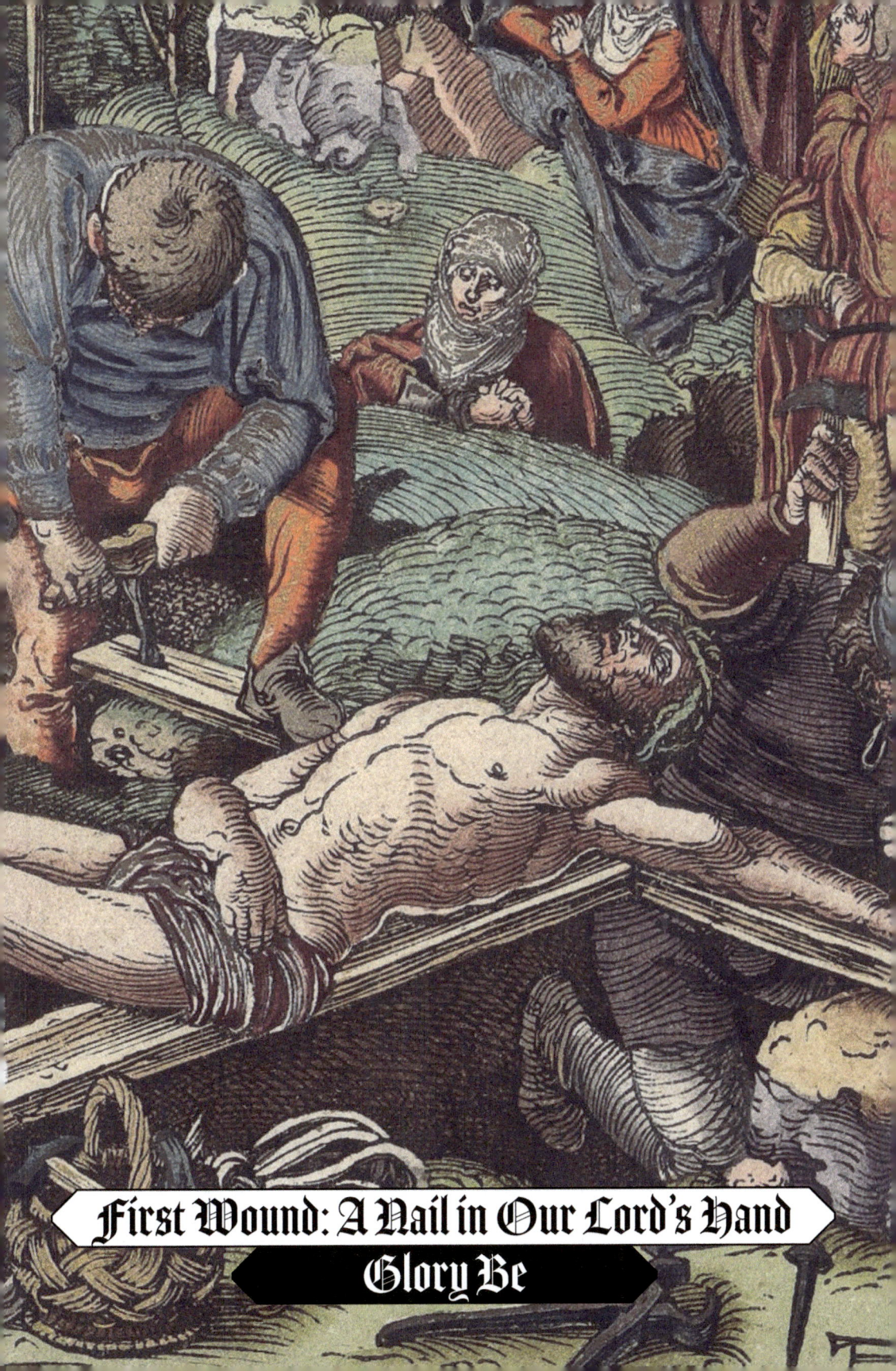

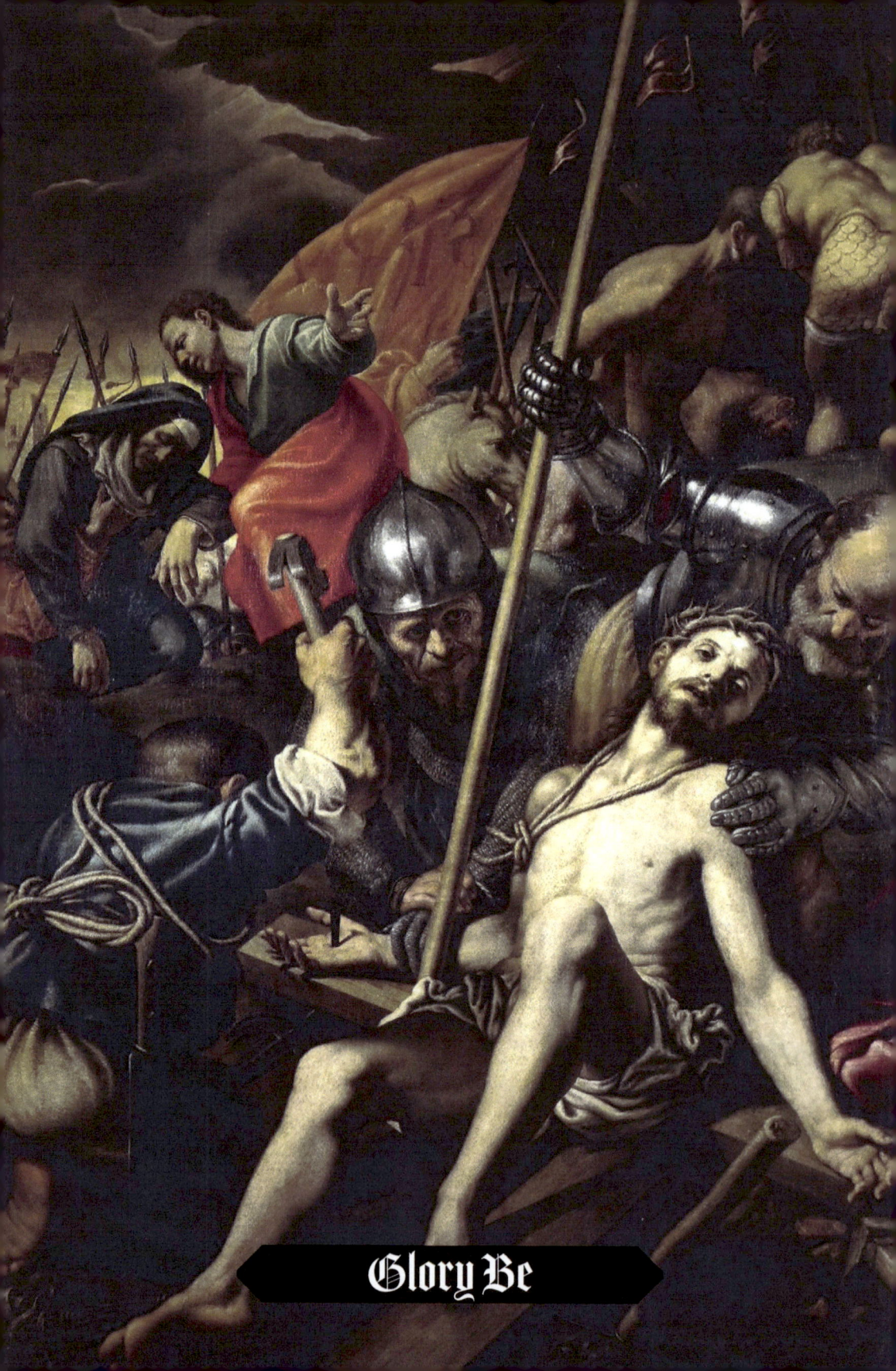

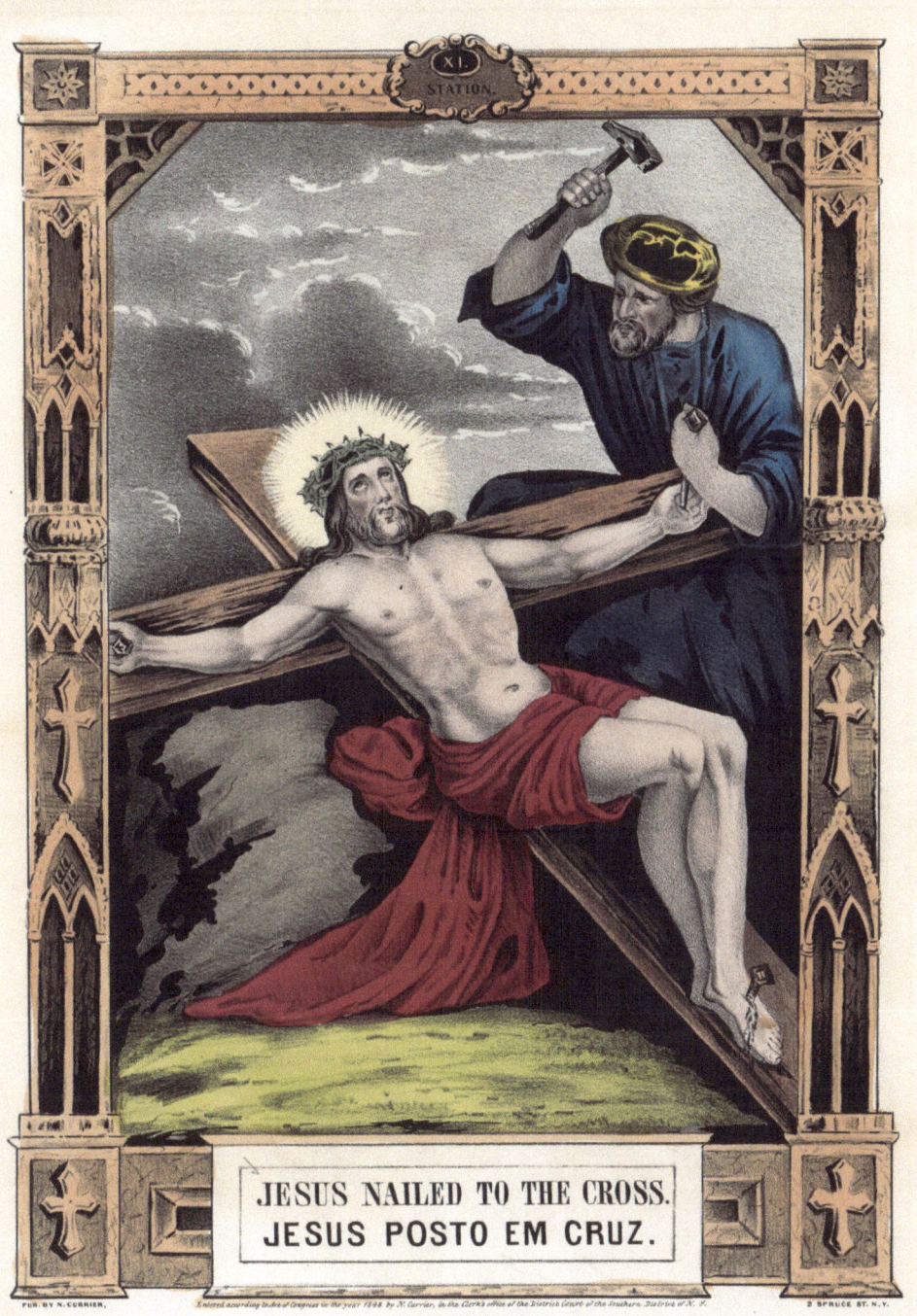

Glory Be

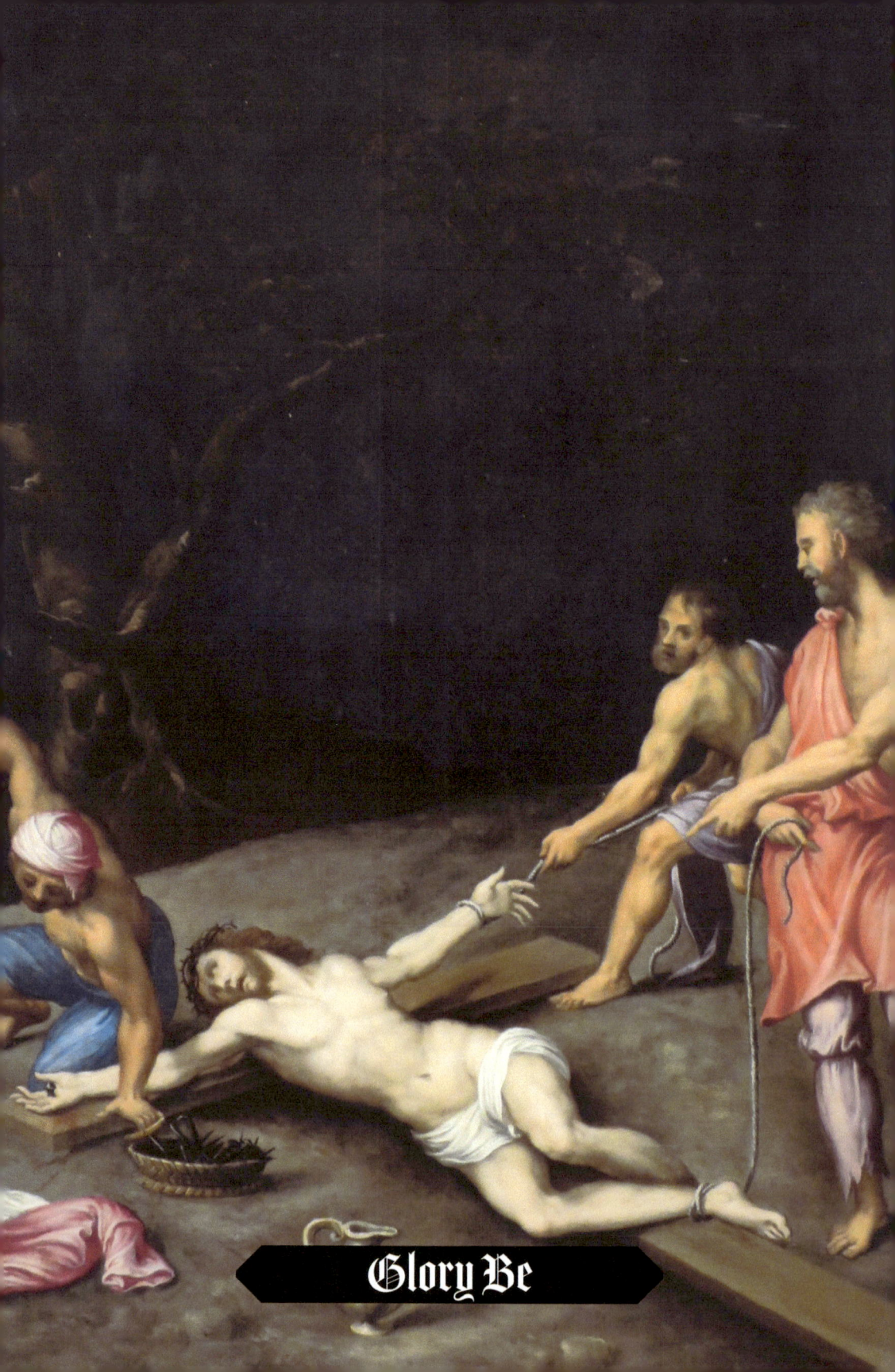

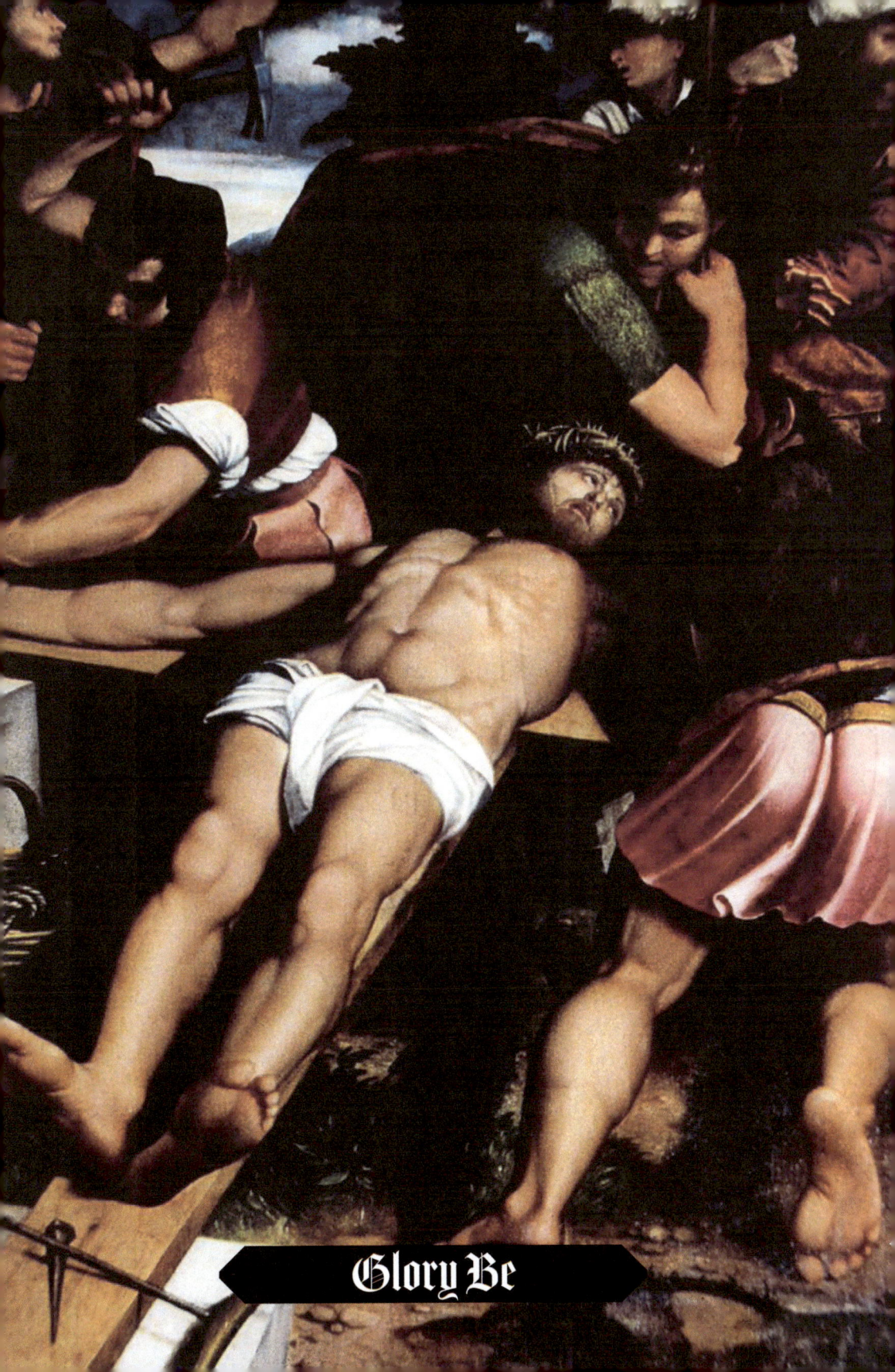

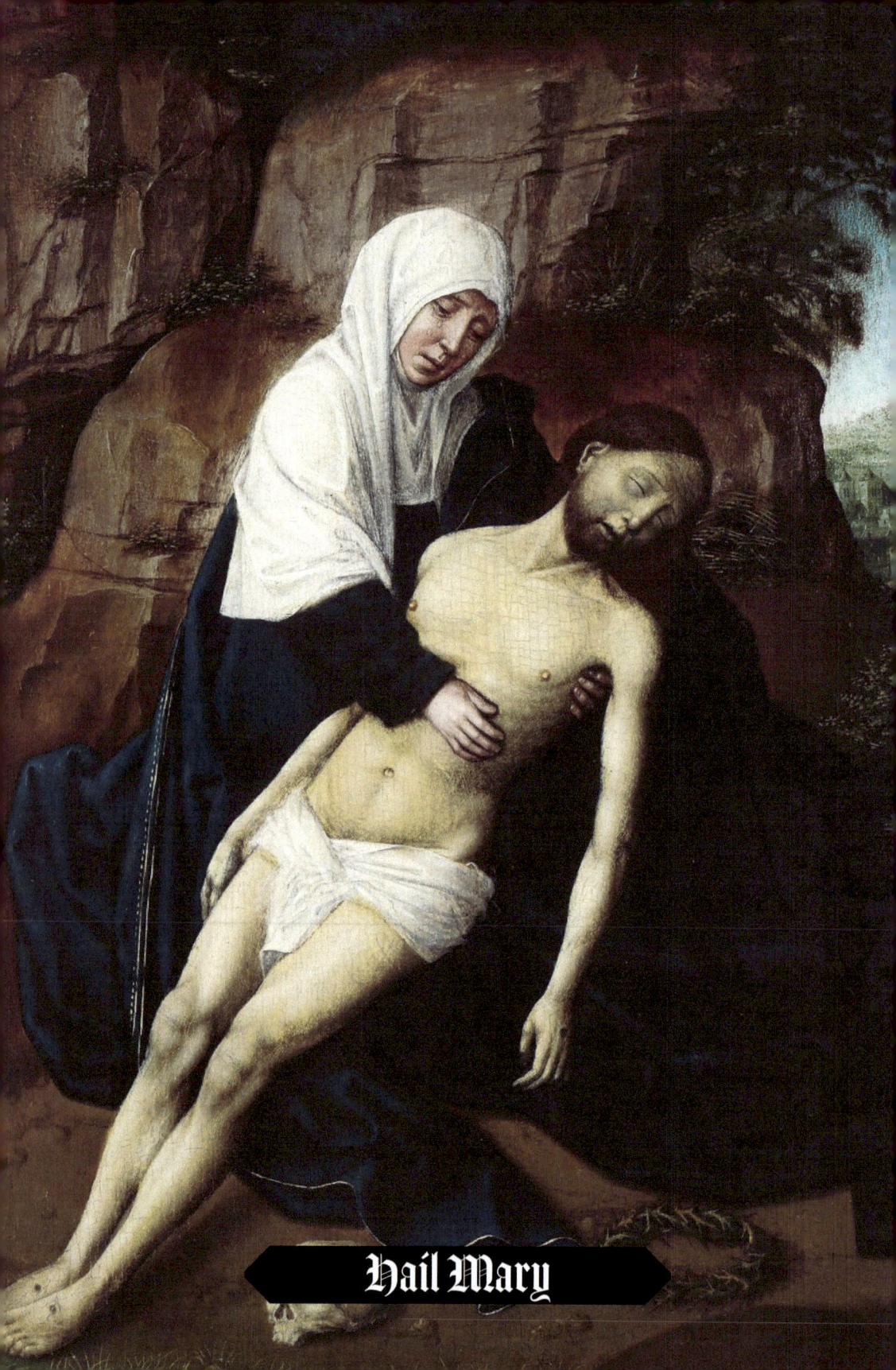

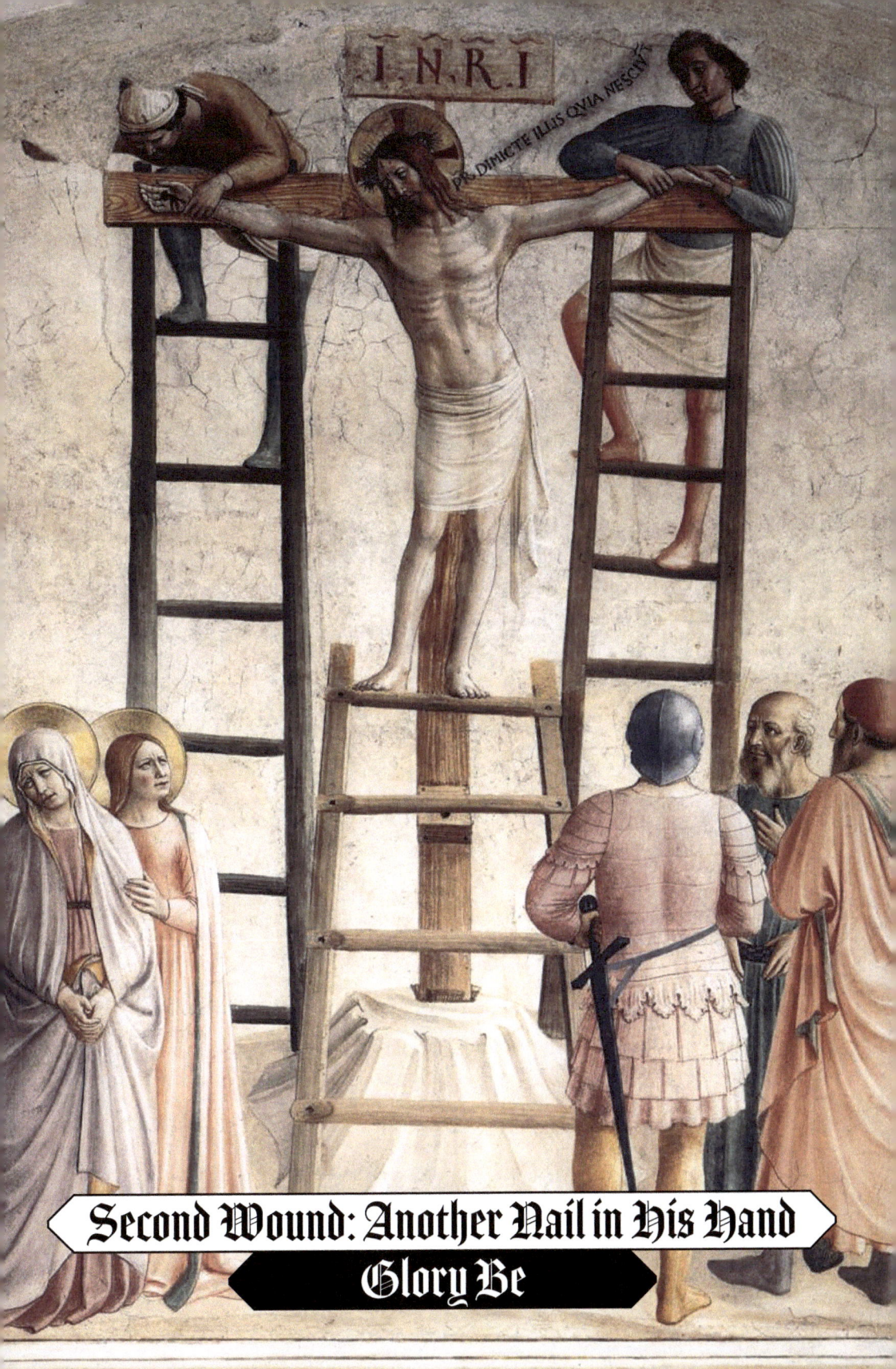

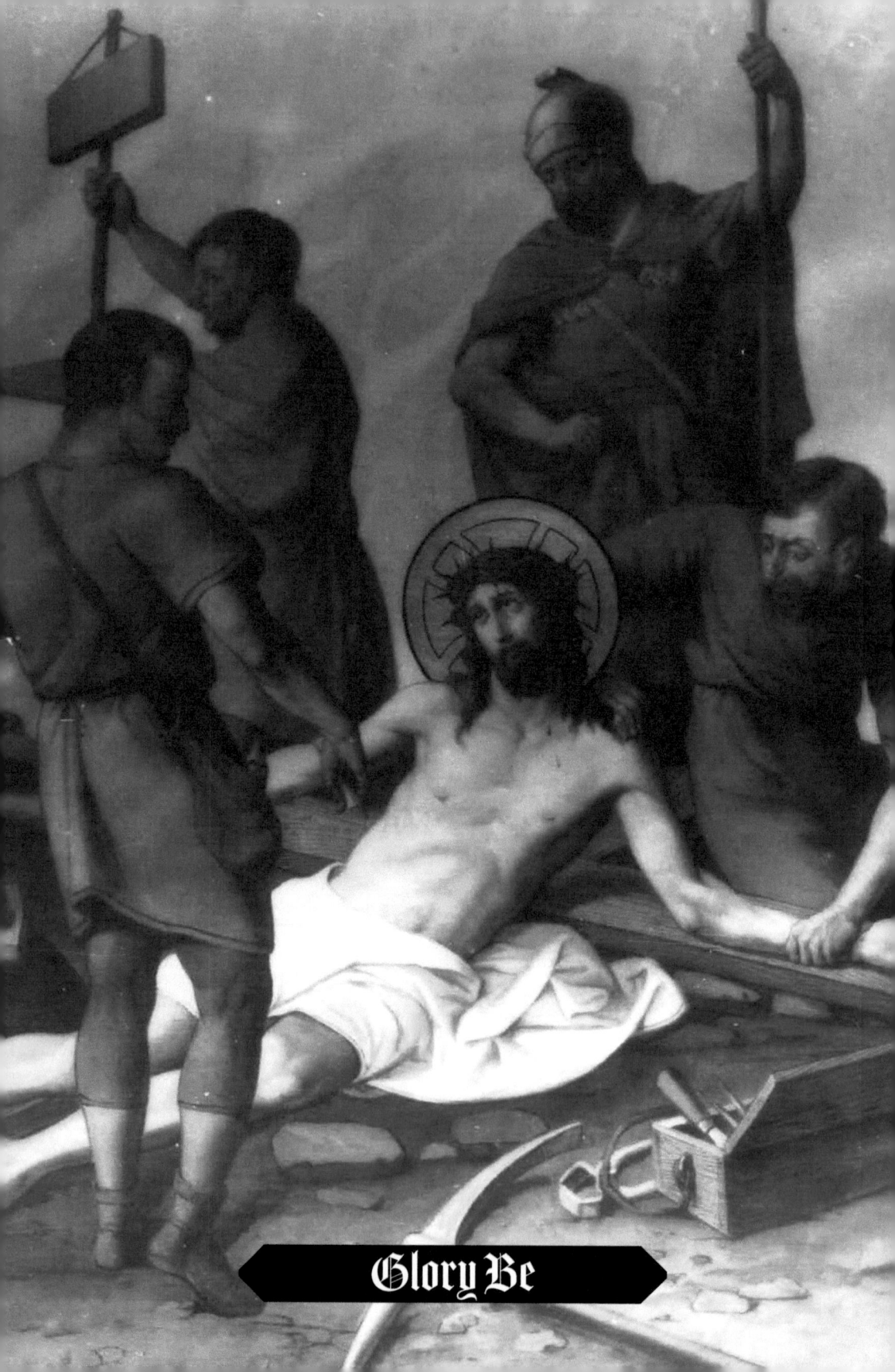

Glory Be

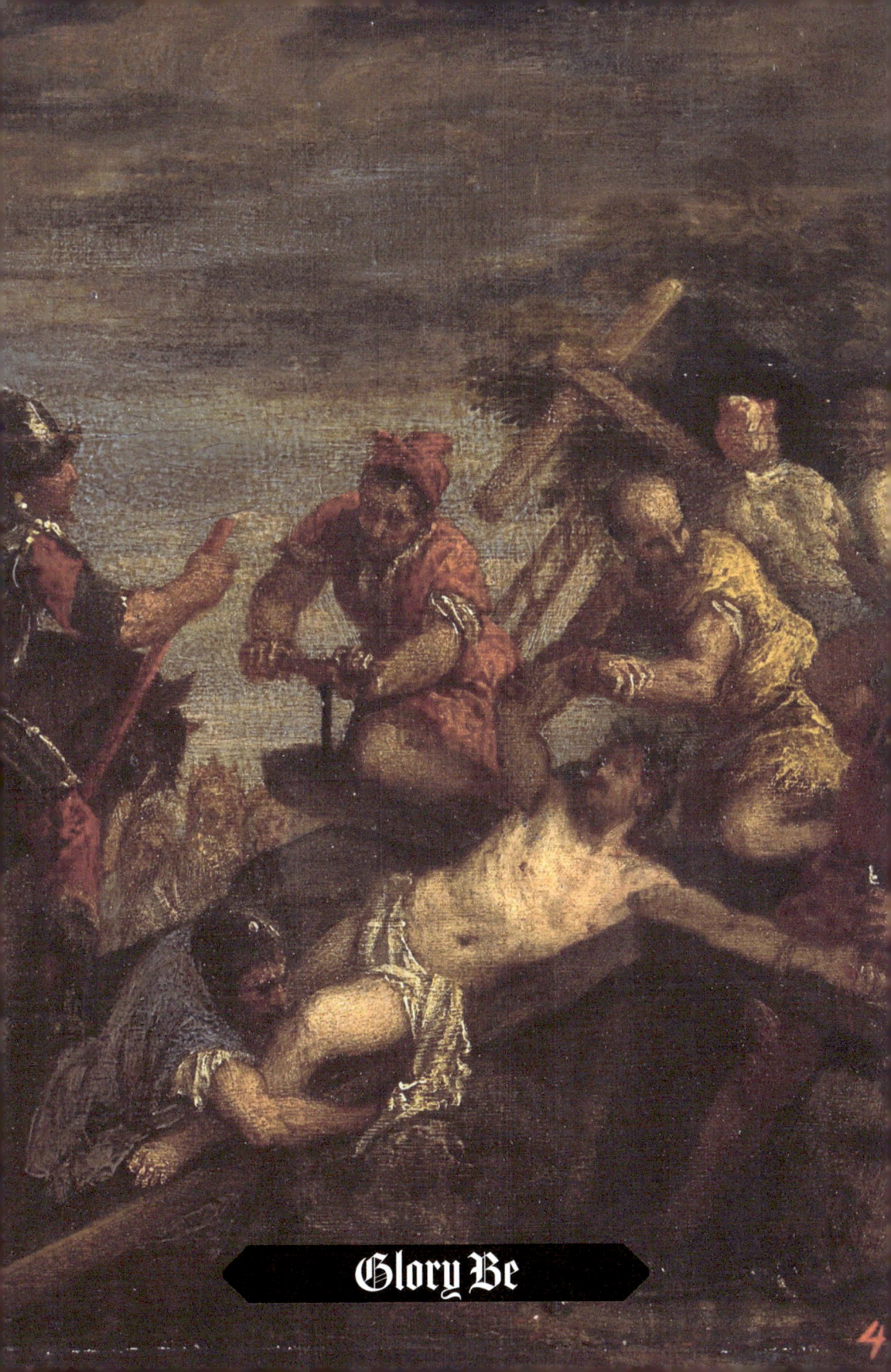

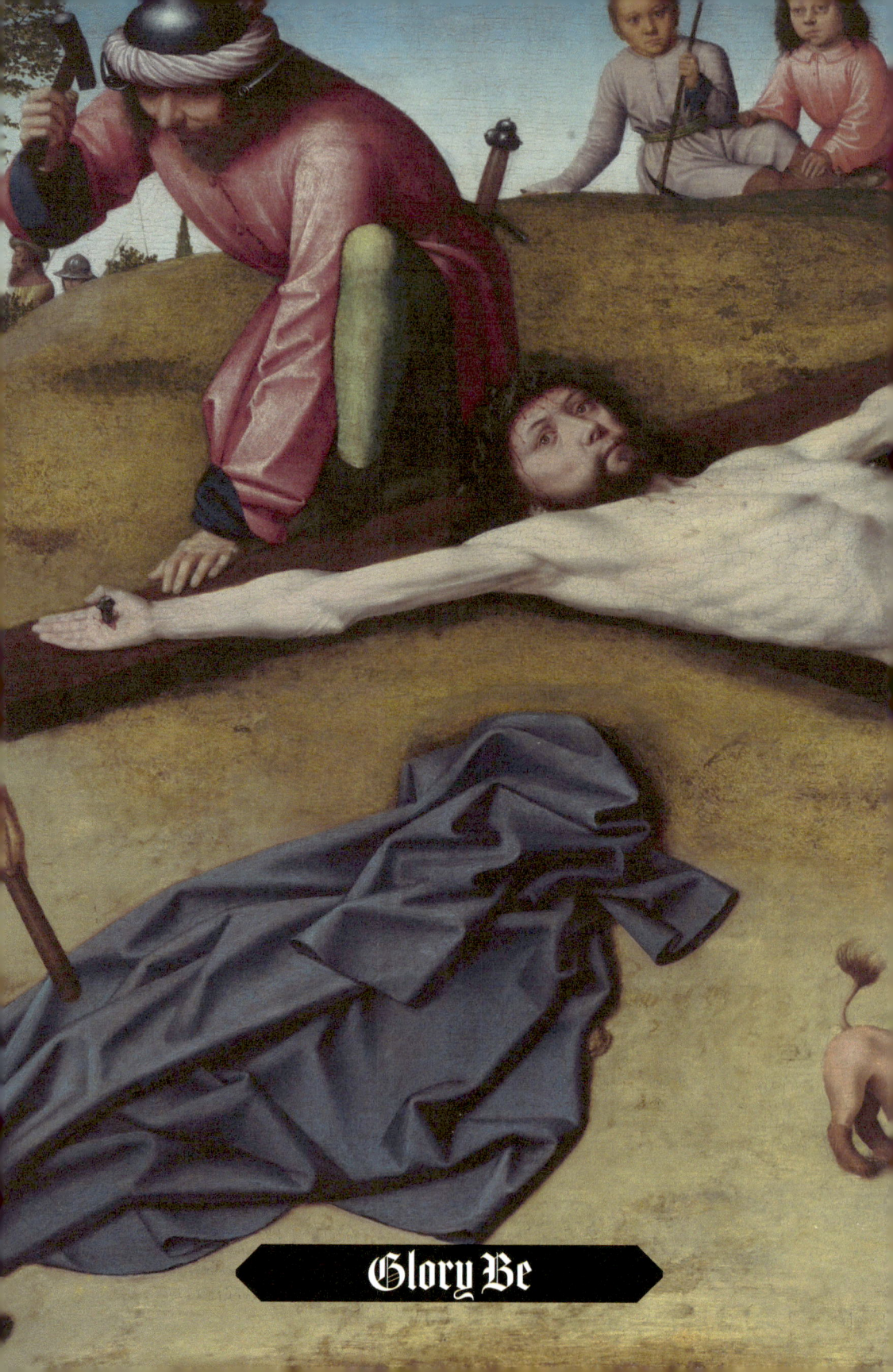

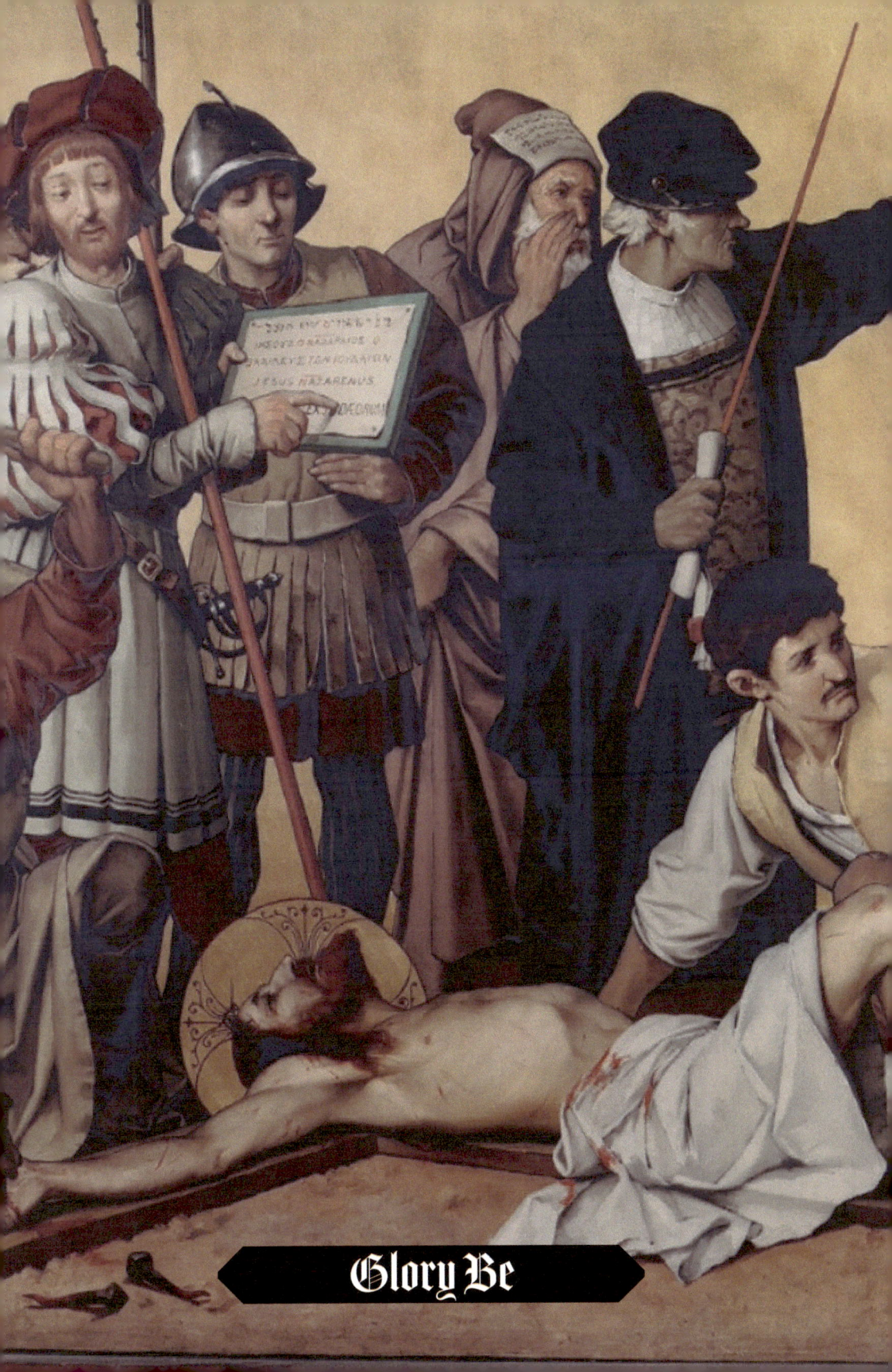

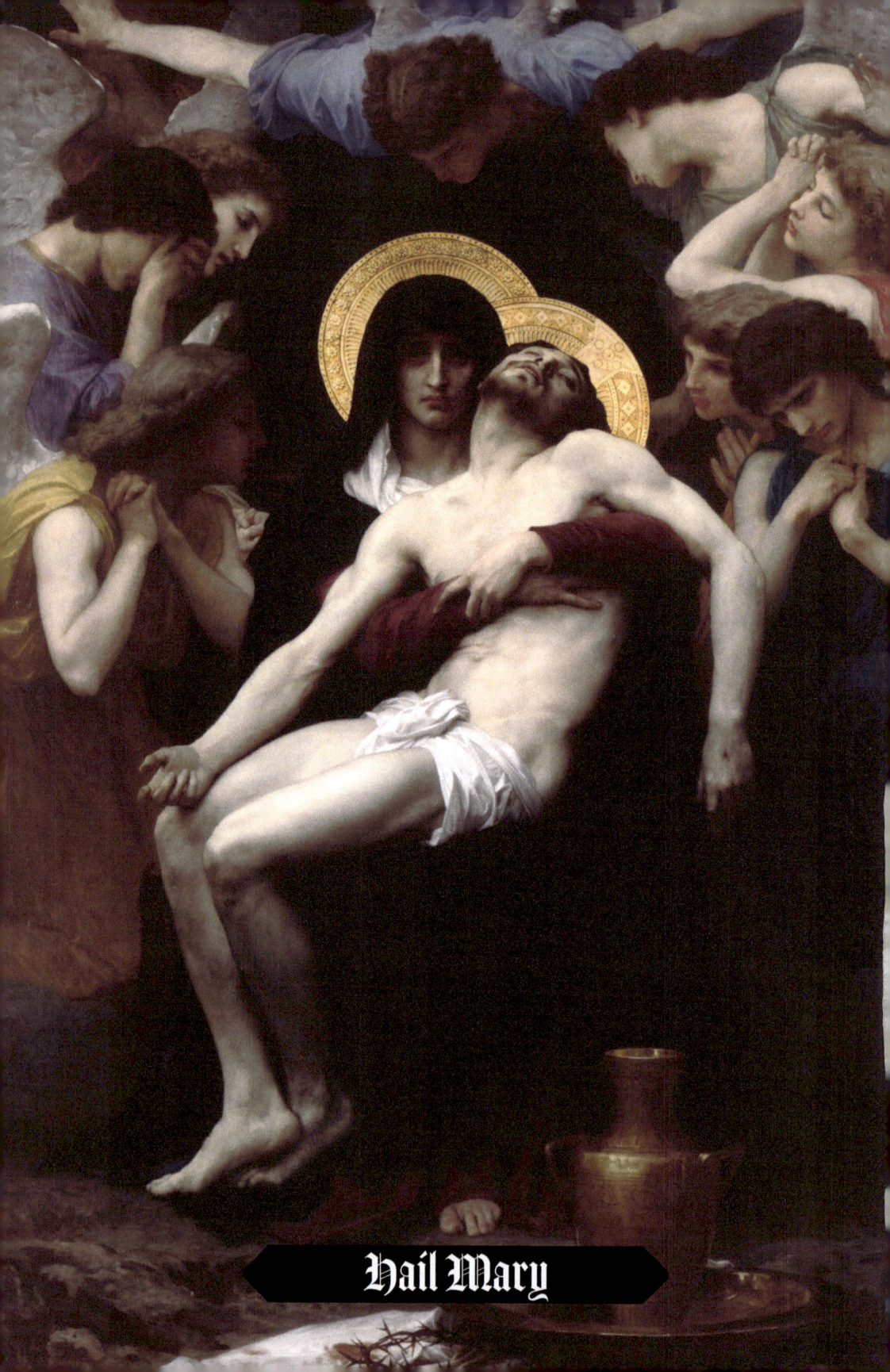

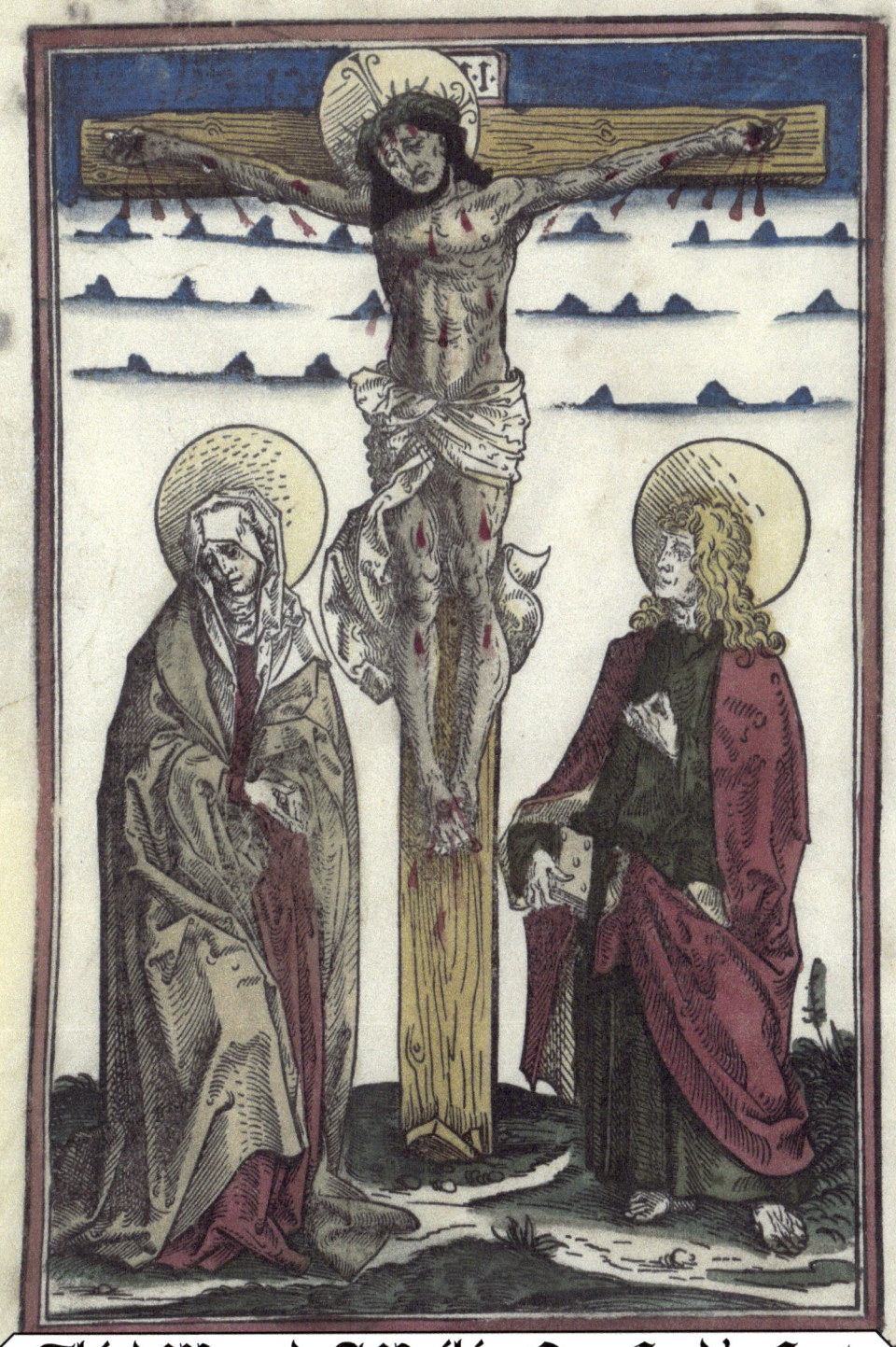

Third Wound: A Nail in Our Lord's Foot
Glory Be

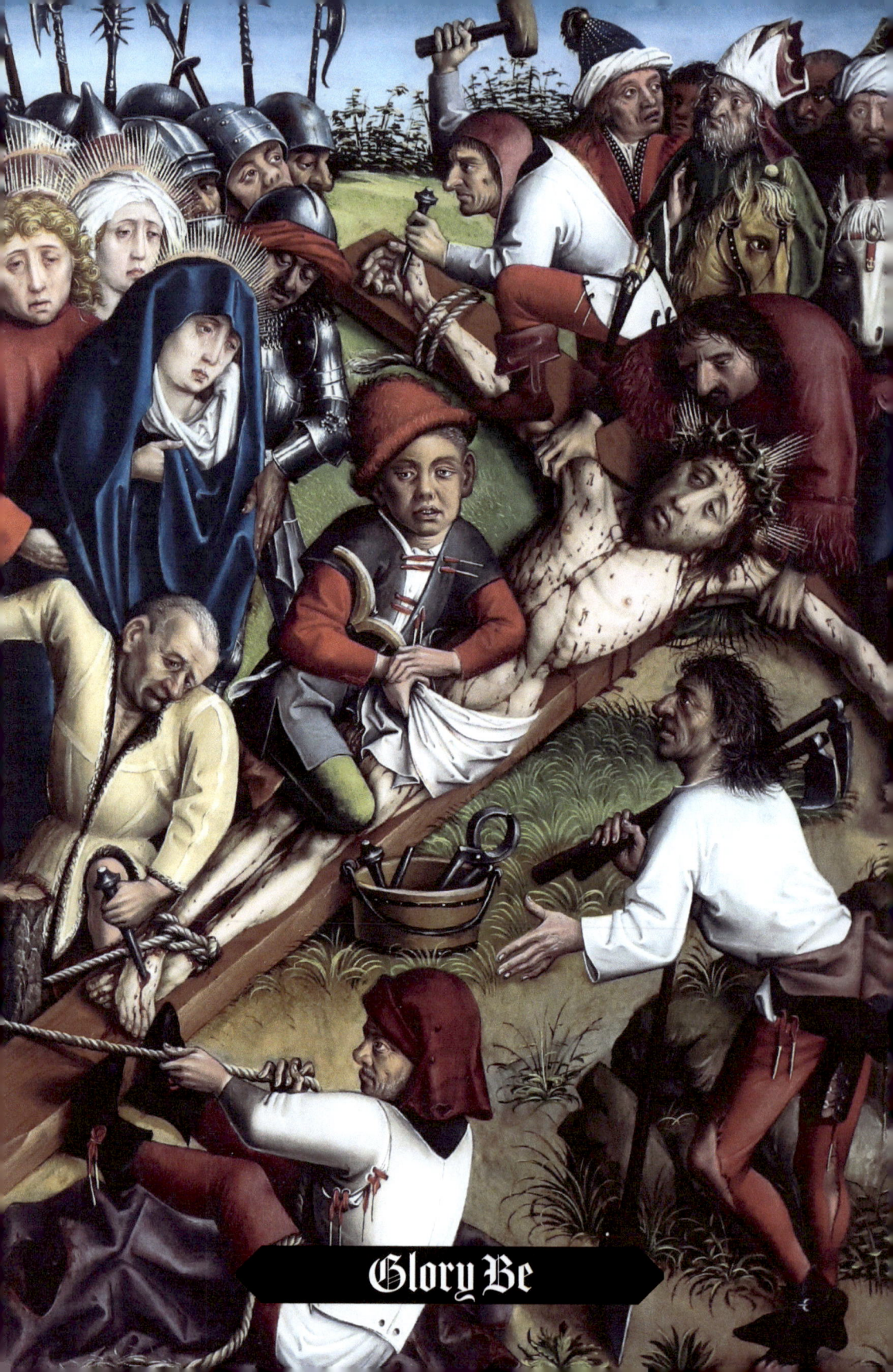
Glory Be

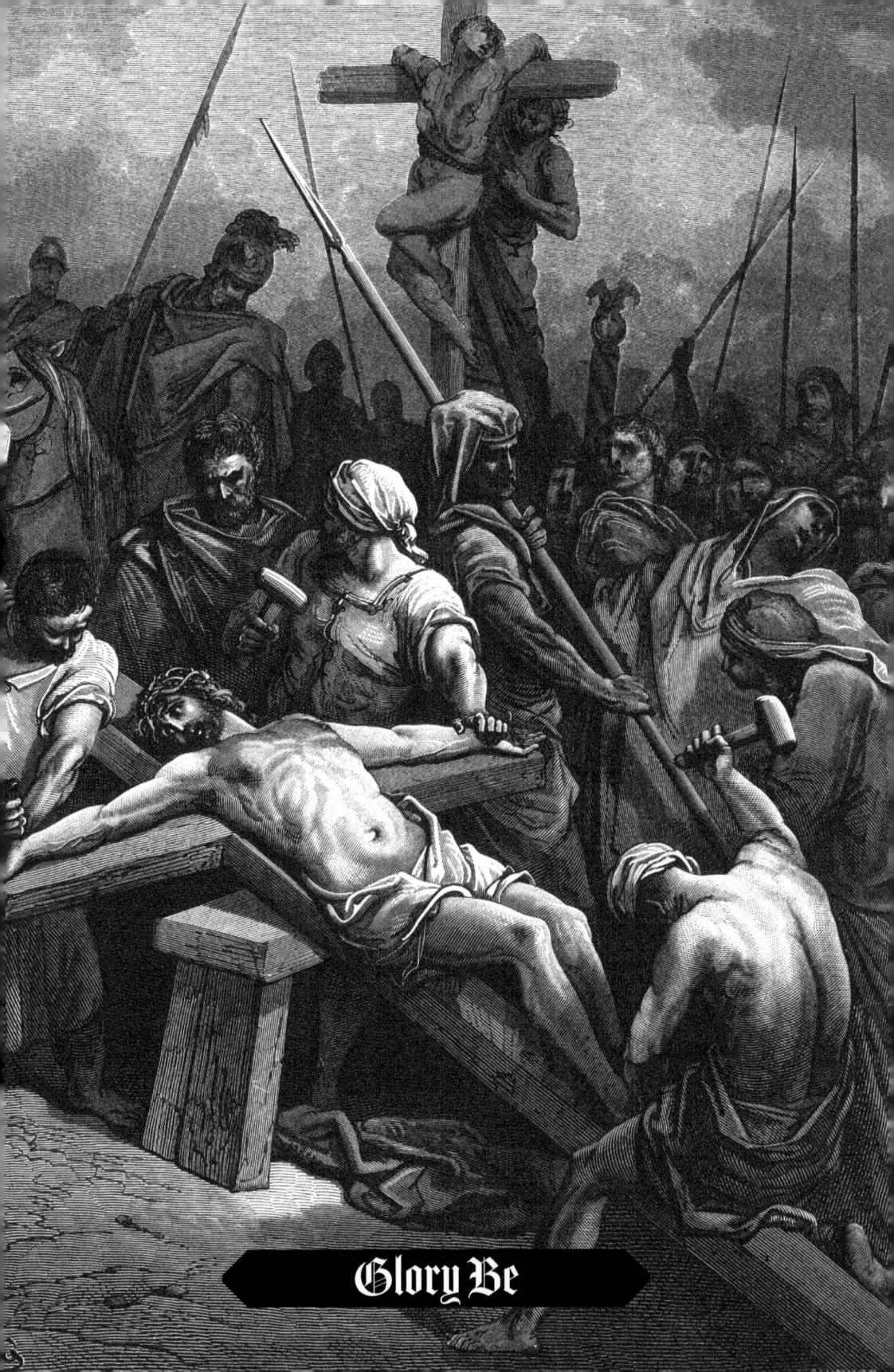

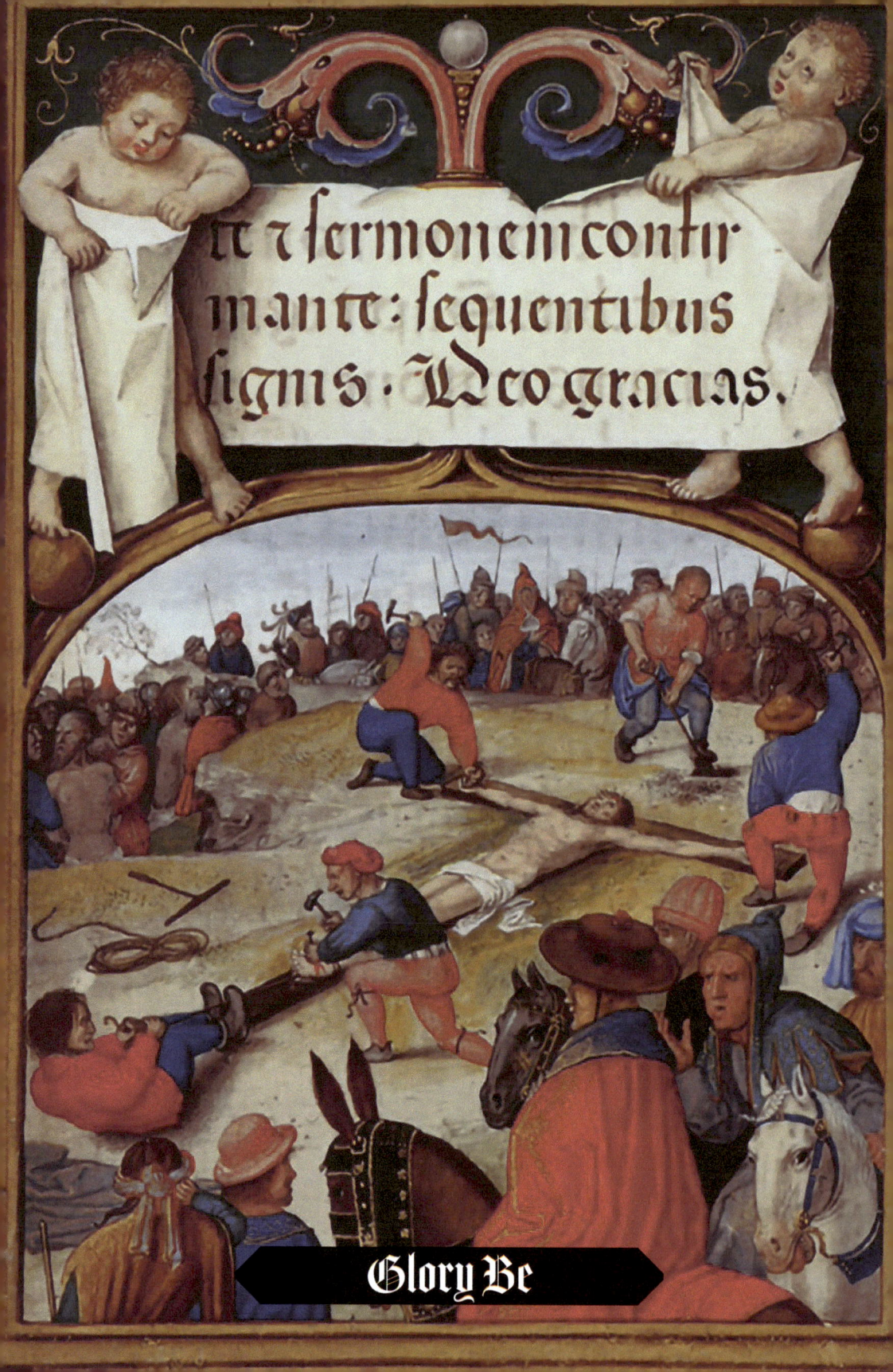

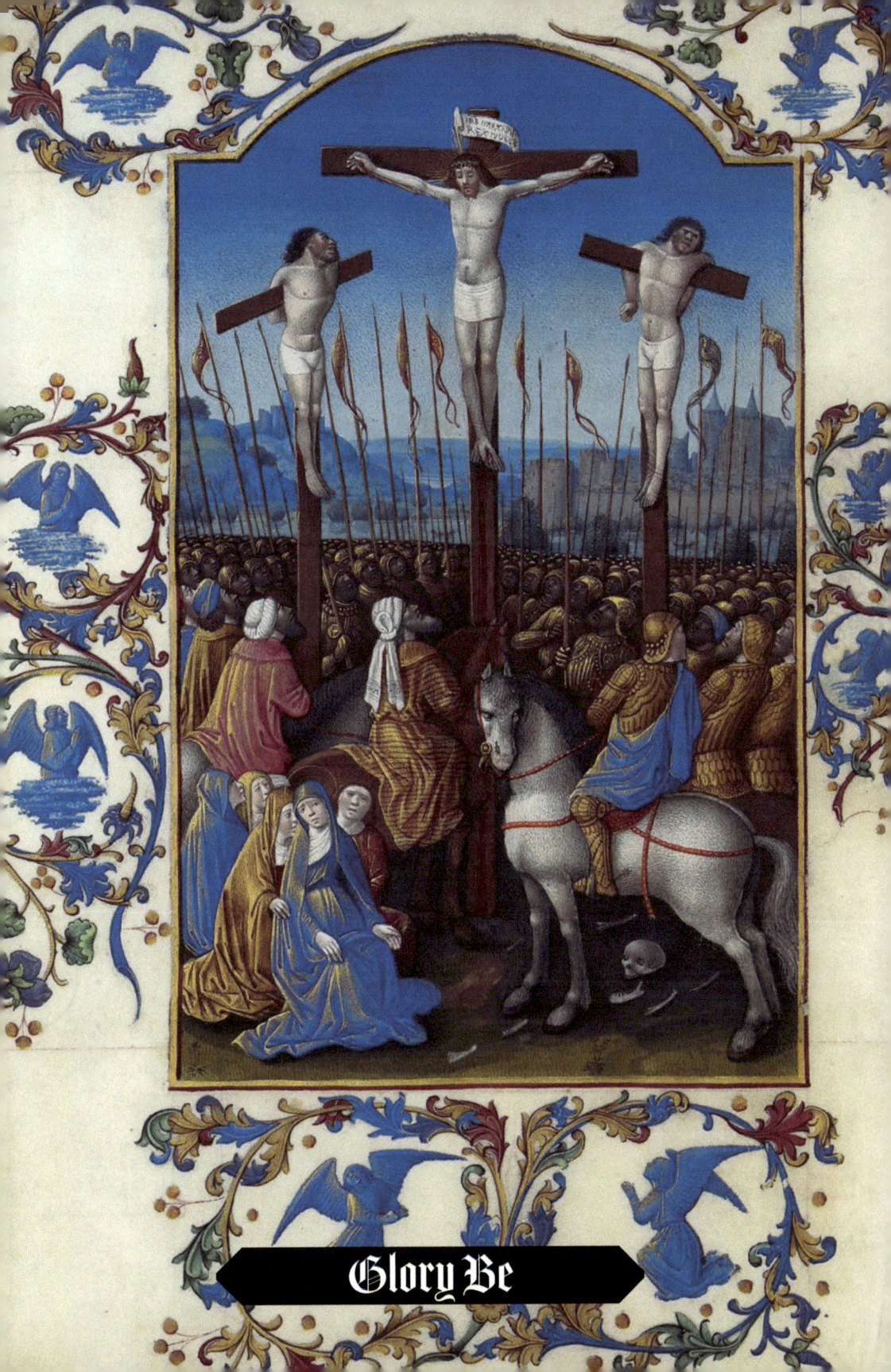

Glory Be

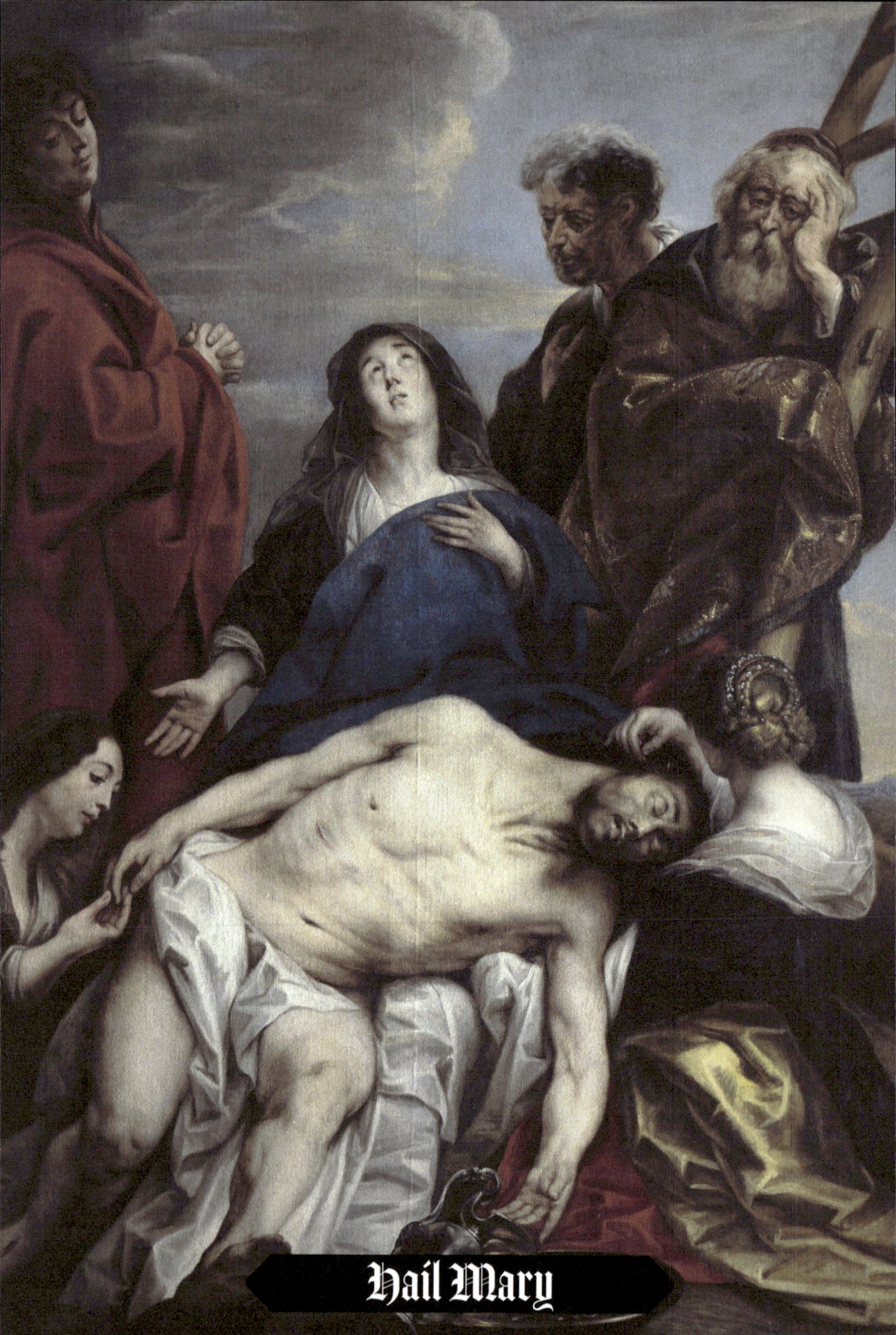

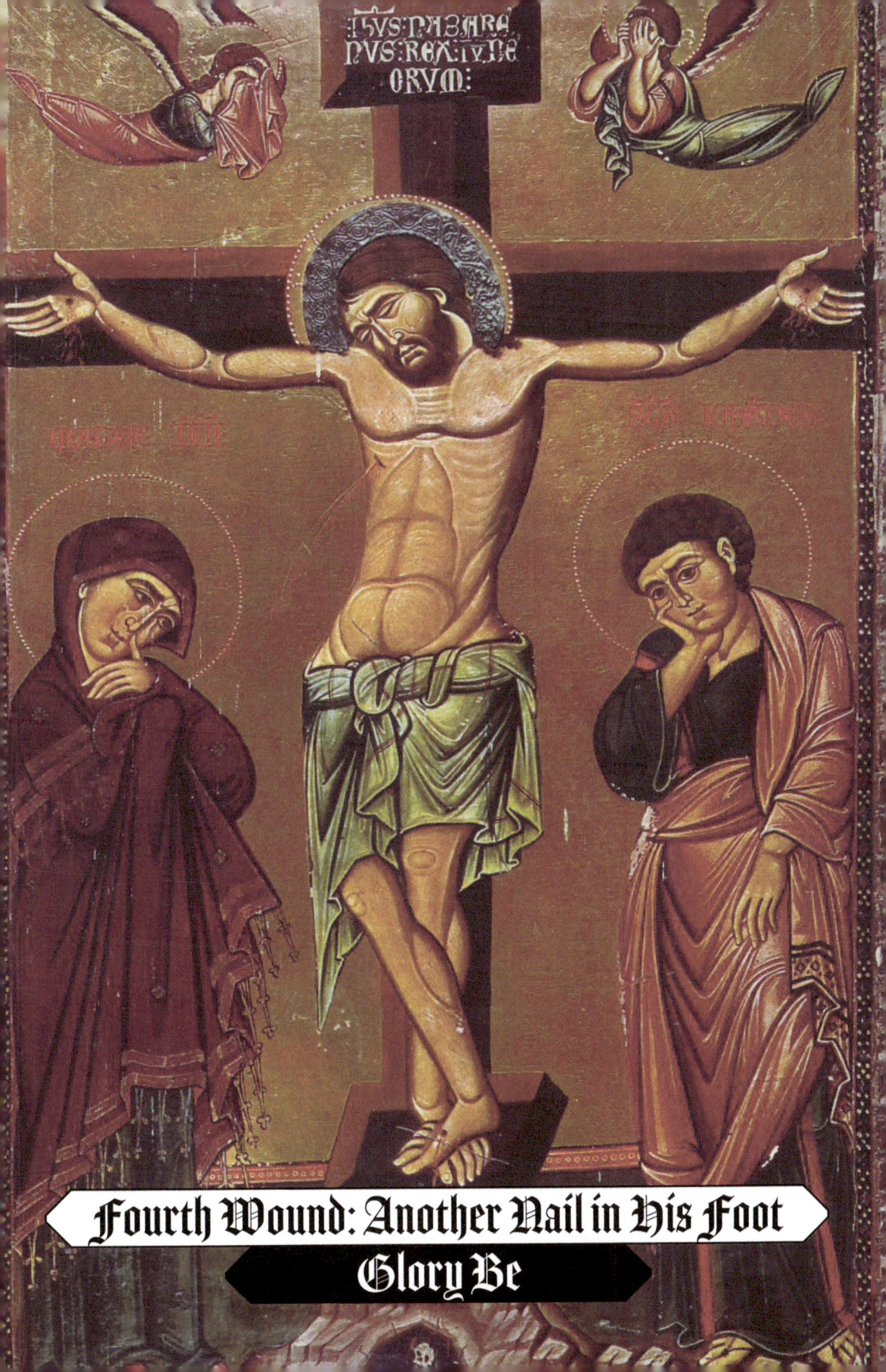

Fourth Wound: Another Nail in His Foot
Glory Be

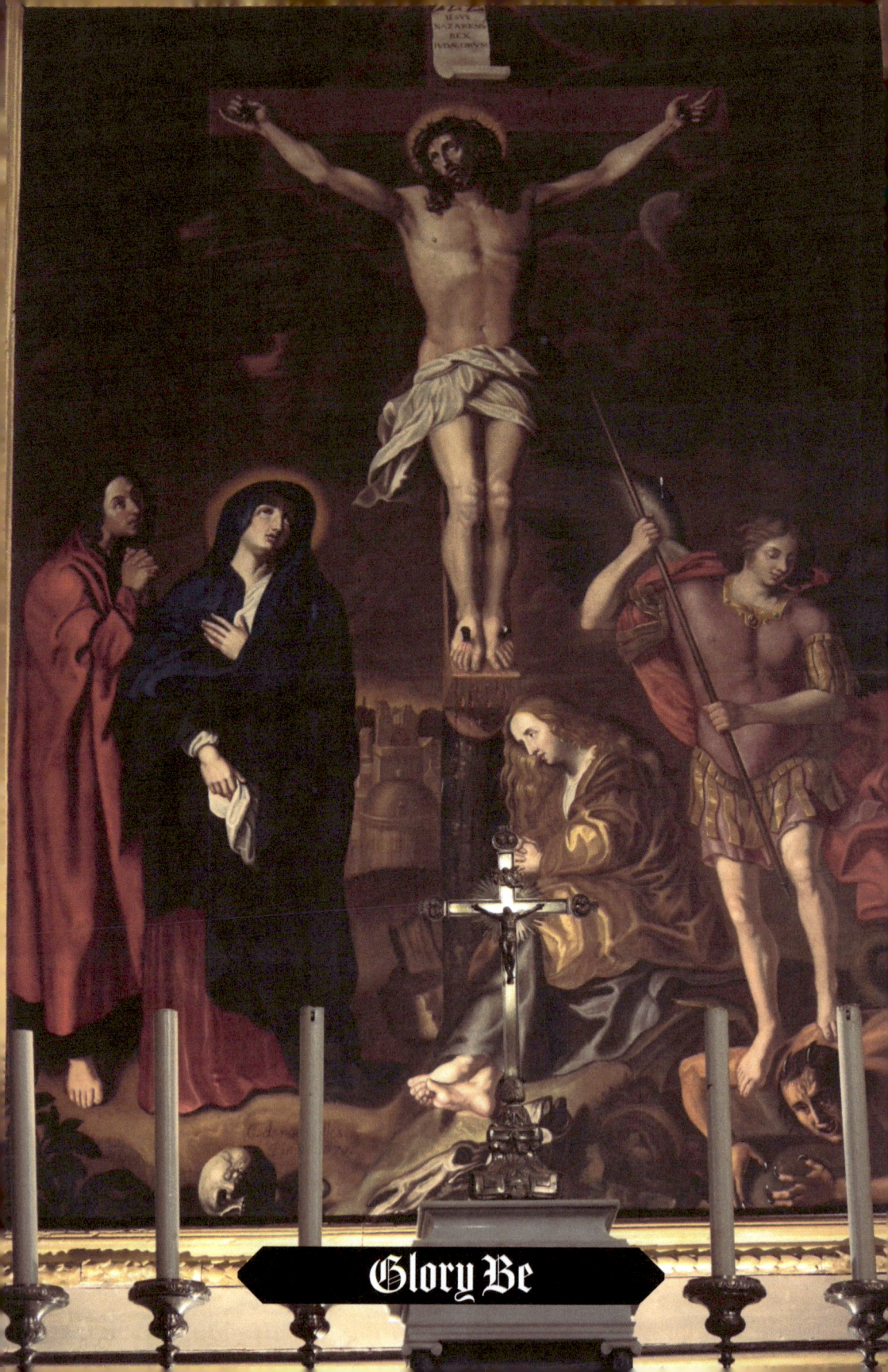

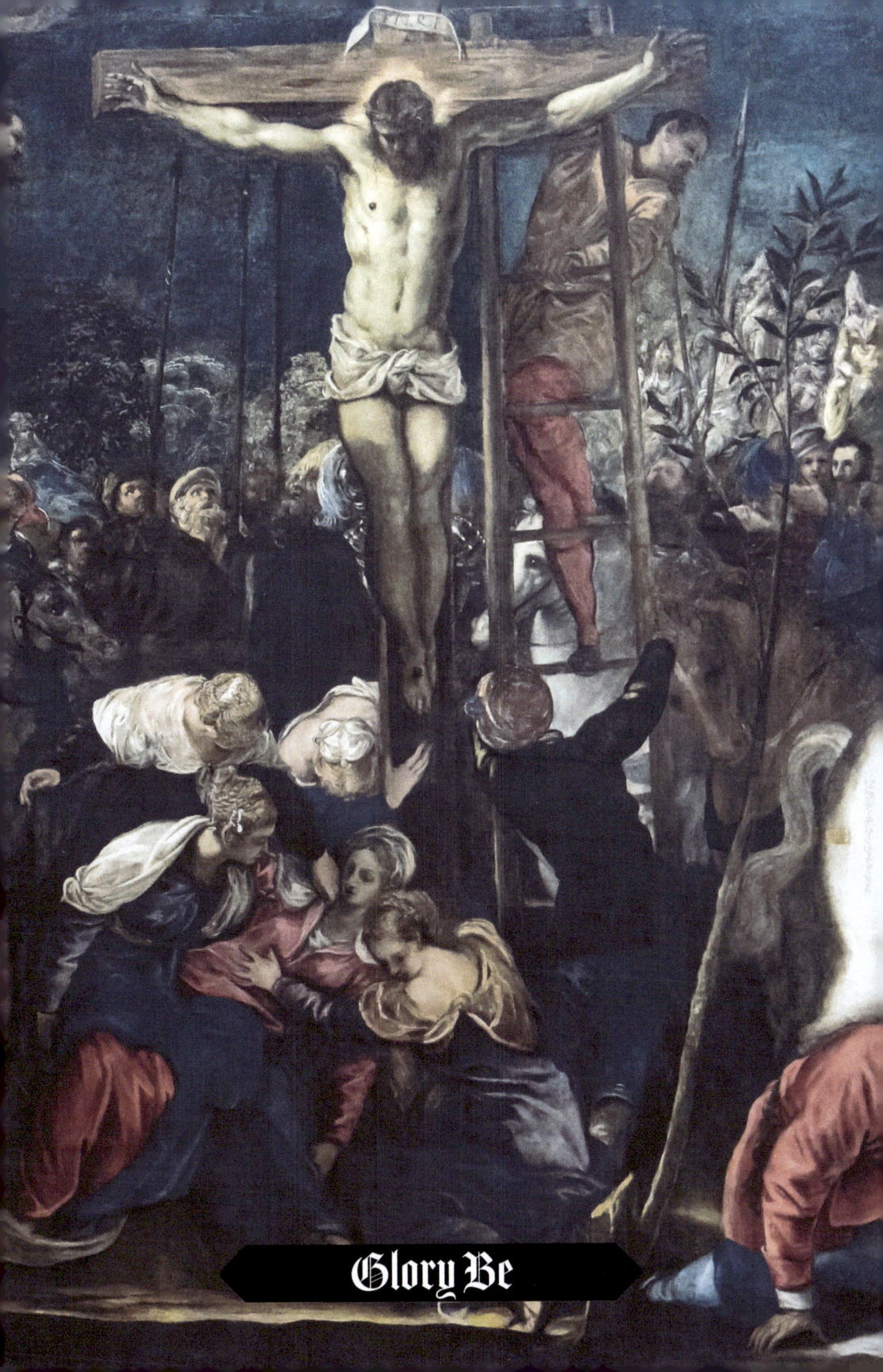

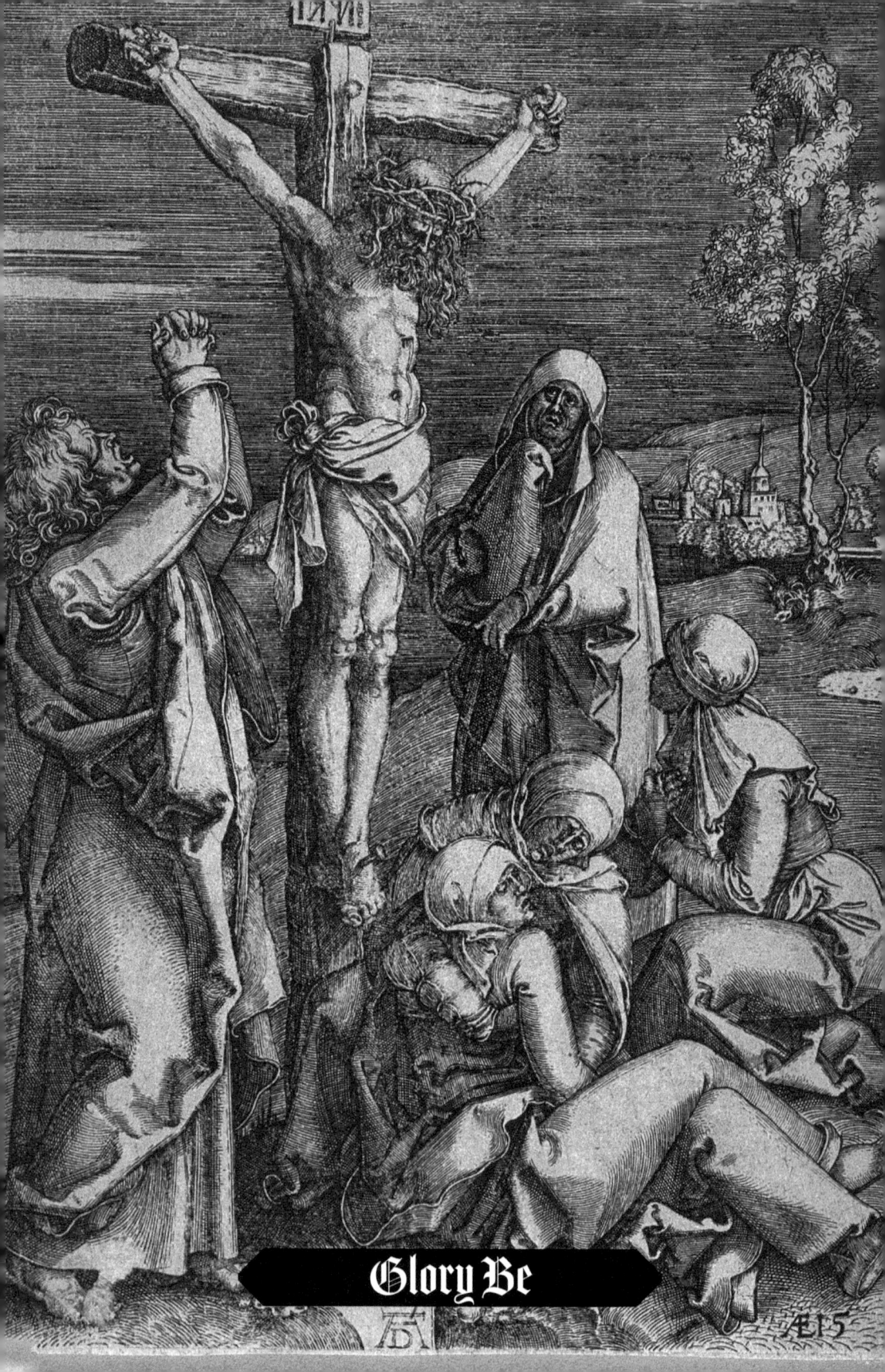

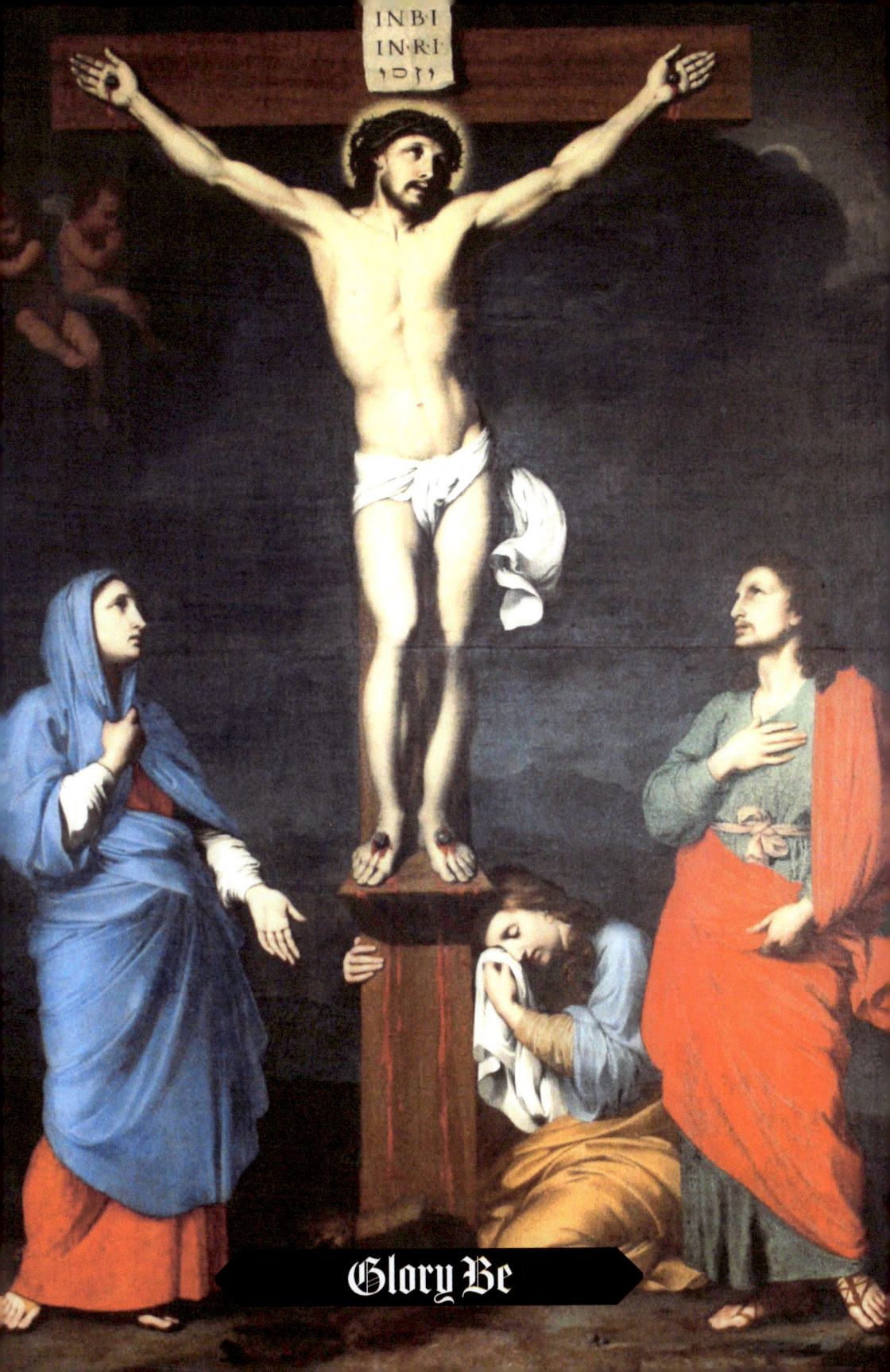

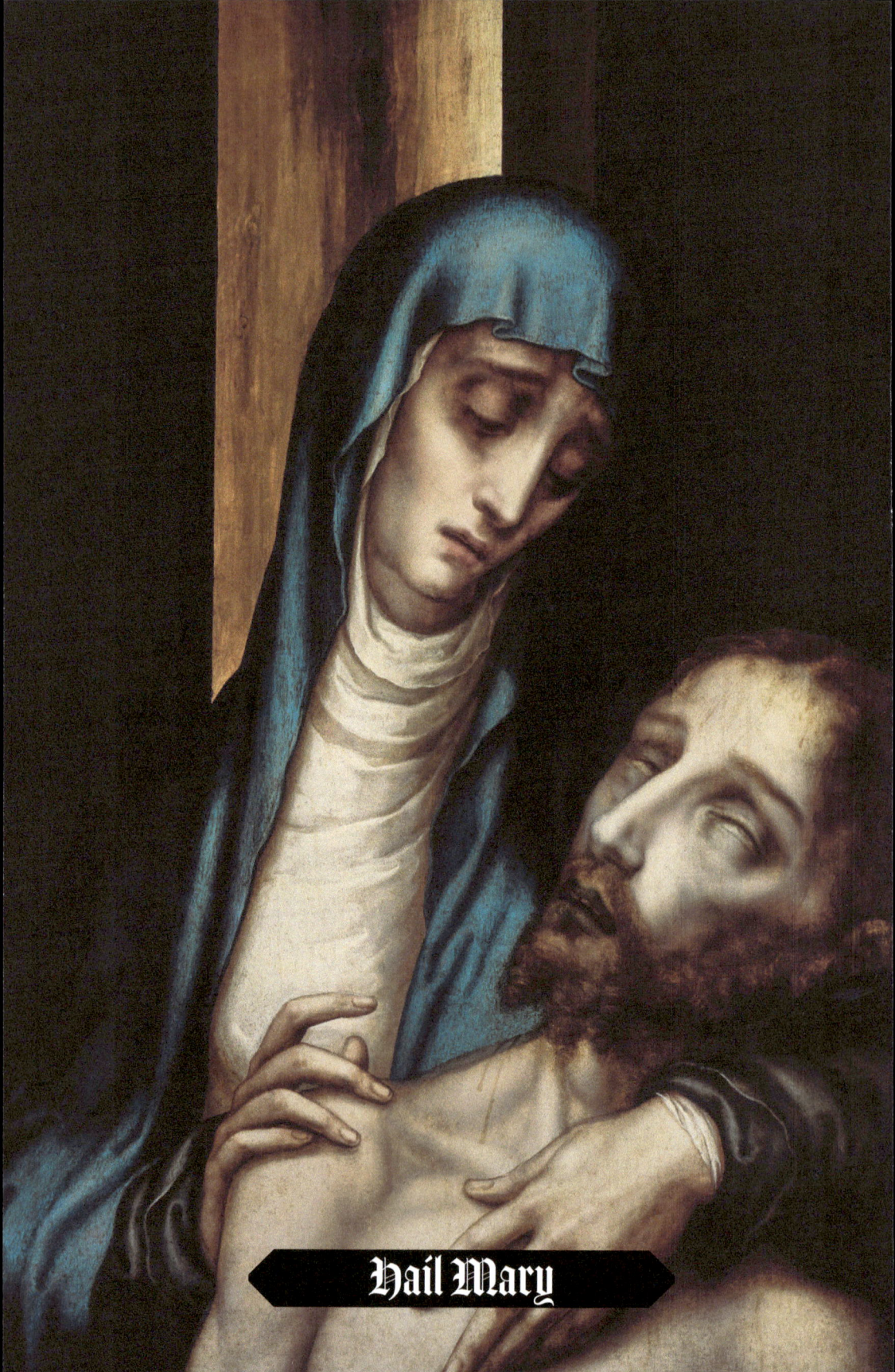

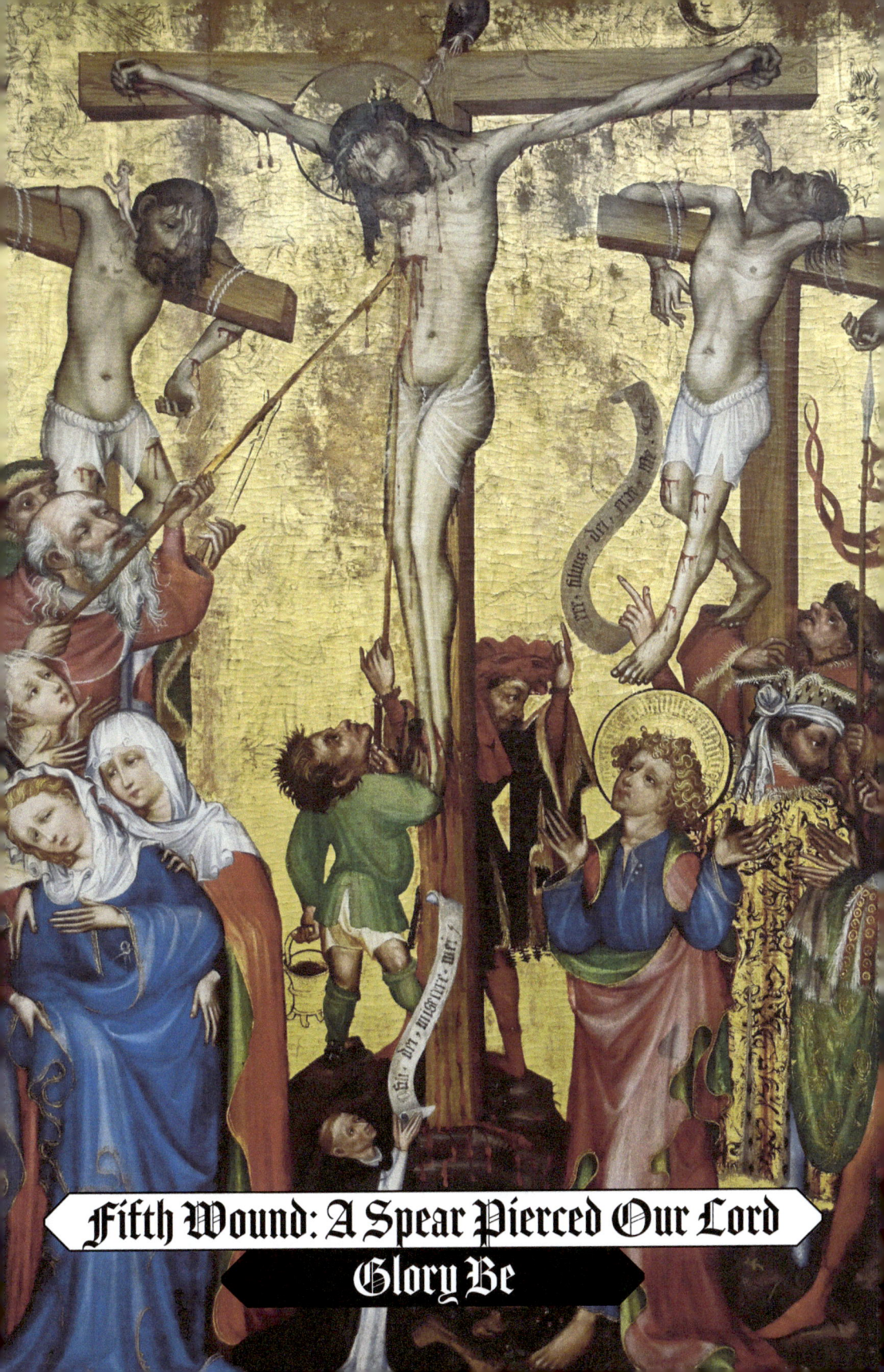

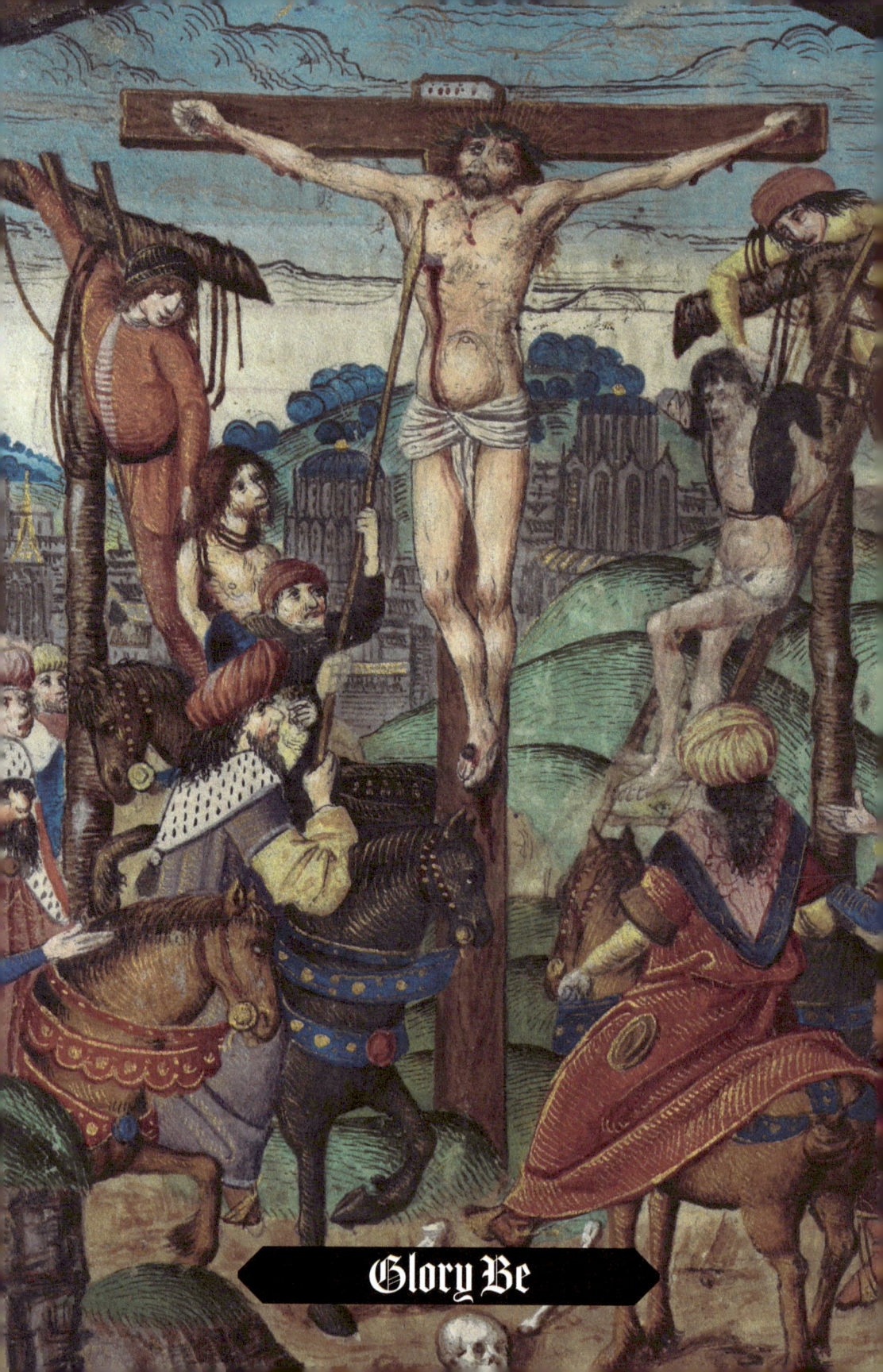

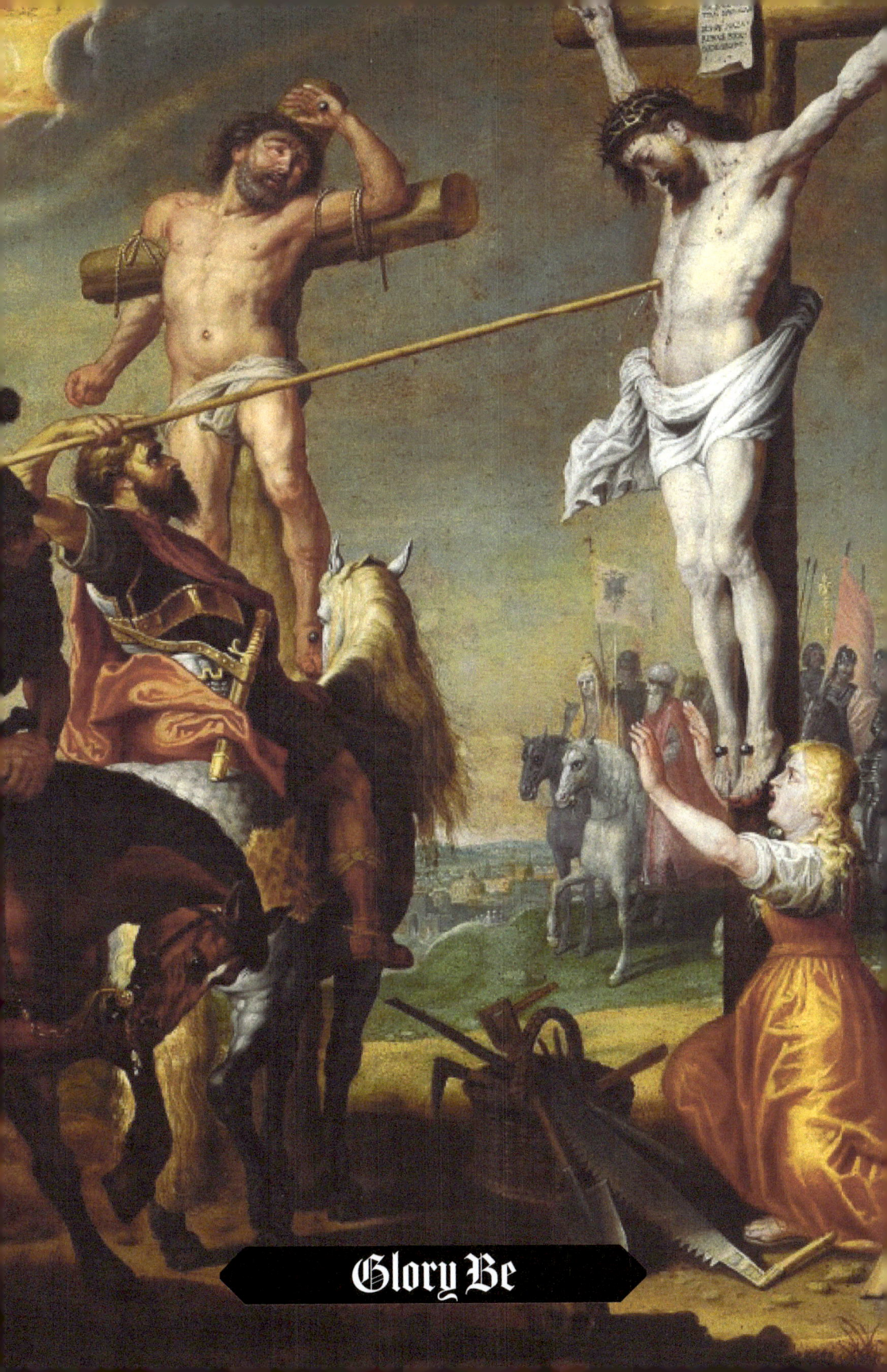
Glory Be

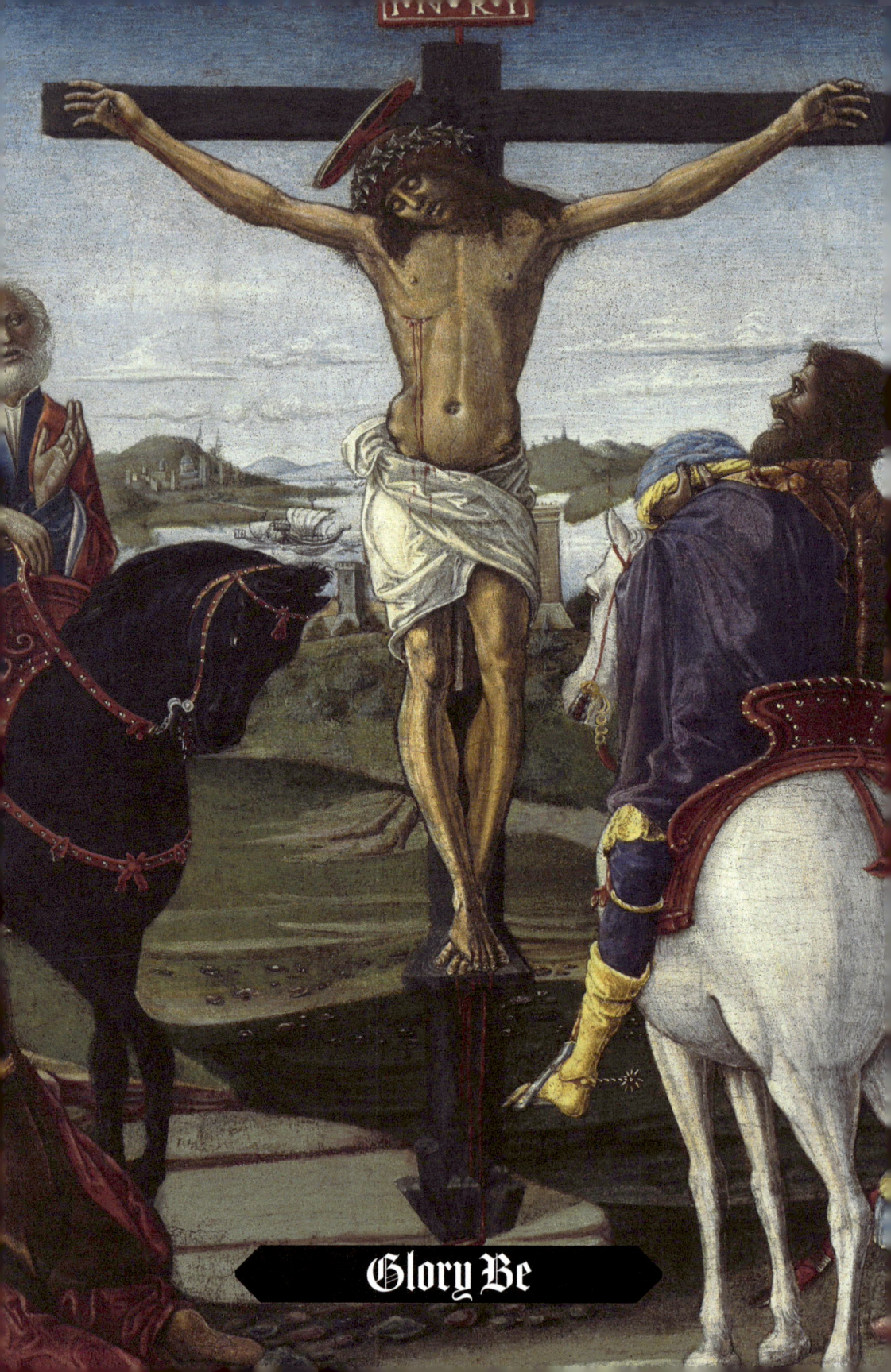

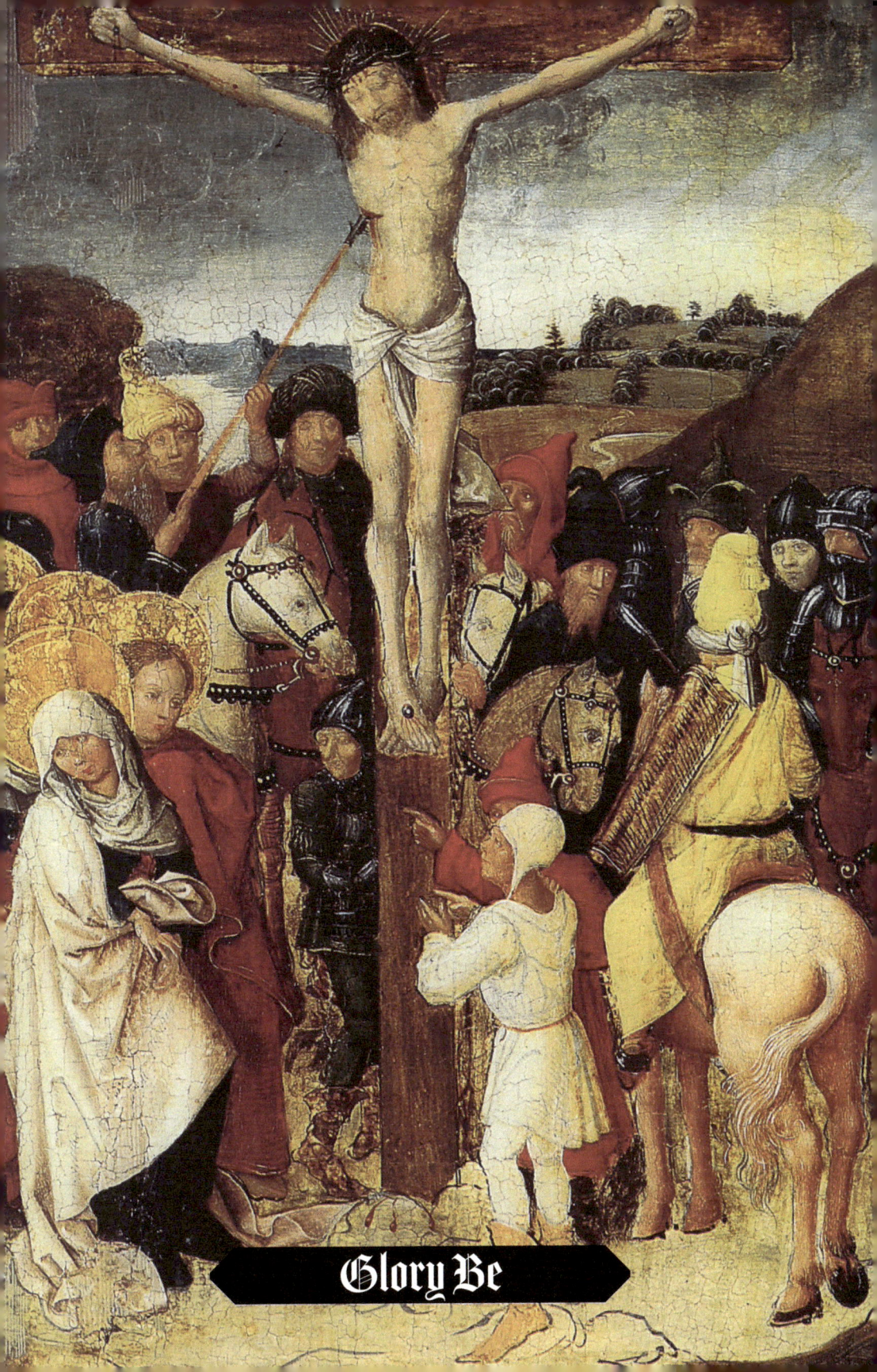
Glory Be

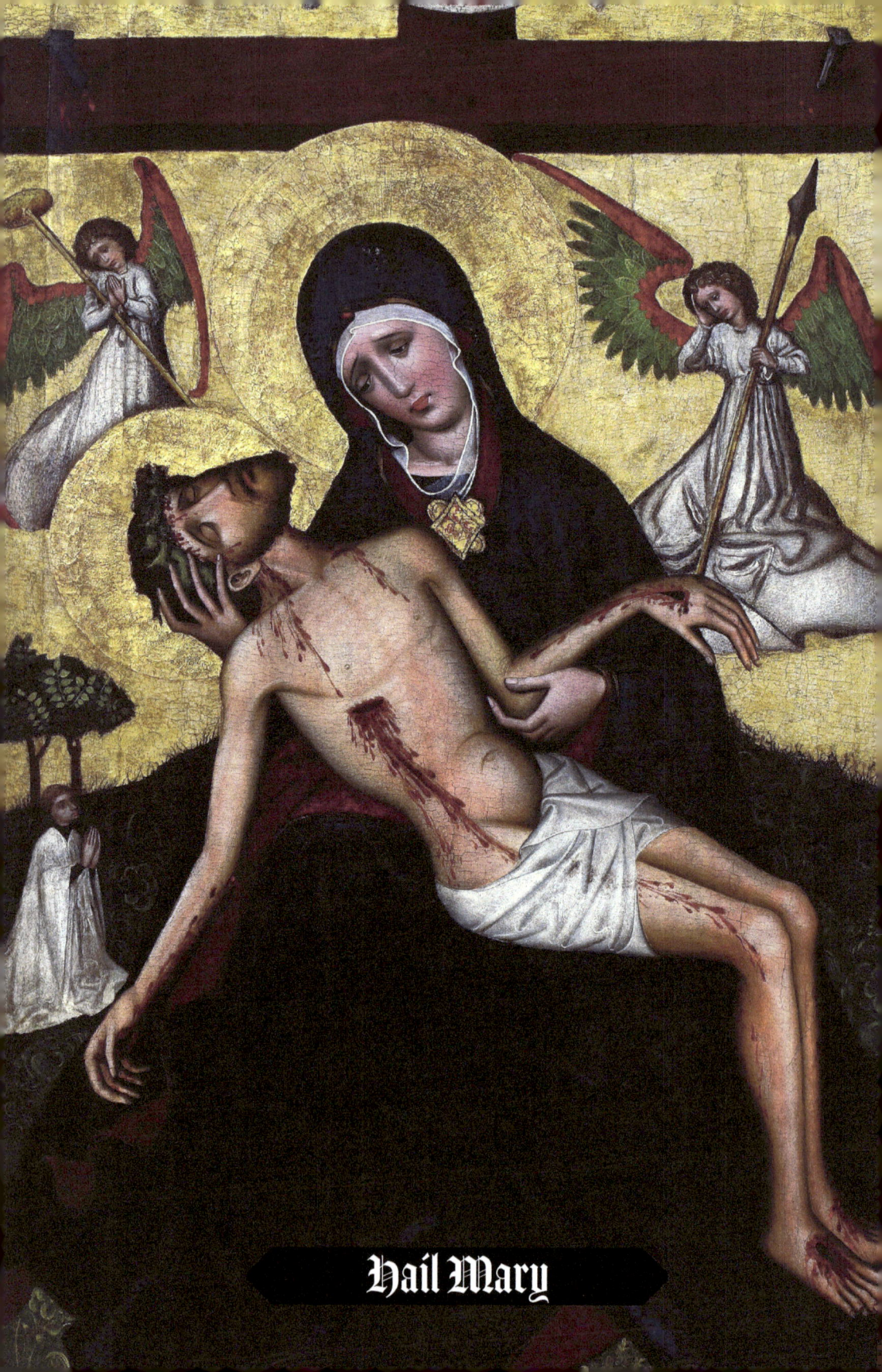

Thank you for purchasing and praying with our books!
Check out our other products and books at casoncatholic.com
+ God Bless +

Please Leave us a Review on Amazon

www.ingramcontent.com/pod-product-compliance
Lightning Source LLC
Chambersburg PA
CBHW040259220526
45473CB00002B/531